Hudson's

BUILDING
AND ENGINEERING
CONTRACTS

Including the Duties and Liabilities of

ARCHITECTS, ENGINEERS AND SURVEYORS

TENTH EDITION

FIRST SUPPLEMENT

BY

I. N. DUNCAN WALLACE, Q.C., M.A. OXON.

of the Middle Temple, Barrister-at-Law

LONDON

SWEET & MAXWELL

1979

Published by
Sweet & Maxwell Limited of
11 New Fetter Lane, London
and printed in Great Britain
by The Eastern Press Ltd. of
London and Reading

SBN 421 25730 **X**

TABLE OF CASES IN SUPPLEMENT

N.B. *References are to pages of main work as set out in margin of this Supplement.*

TABLE OF CASES IN SUPPLEMENT

TABLE OF CASES IN SUPPLEMENT

TABLE OF CASES IN SUPPLEMENT

TABLE OF CASES IN SUPPLEMENT

Table of Cases in Supplement

TABLE OF STATUTES IN SUPPLEMENT

N.B. *References are to pages of main work as set out in margin of this Supplement.*

INTRODUCTION

THIS Supplement is designed to cover all the more important cases from 1970 until early 1978 in England and in the Commonwealth and South African jurisdictions. It will be seen that it also contains a small amount of United States material, being a part of the fruits of two delightful periods in successive years spent as a visiting scholar at the Law School at Boalt Hall in the University of California at Berkeley, to the Dean and Faculty of which I must express my sincere appreciation and indebtedness for their help and kindness.

I would like particularly to express my gratitude to Professor Justin Sweet who was responsible for my being invited in the first instance; to Mr. Tom Reynolds, as Librarian, for his quite outstanding kindness and professionalism in guiding me through the maze of the available literature and reports in his superbly equipped and organised Library; and to the Dean and his staff for so generously making an office available to me.

It is intended that the forthcoming Eleventh Edition of Hudson should have a fairly substantial United States content, but the major task of research and selection involved in an examination of the mountain of American reported material, together with the somewhat unpredictable nature of other commitments, means that the Eleventh Edition is not likely to be published for two or three years. The present Supplement in fact contains all the views and material (other than more United States material and, of course, further new cases or developments elsewhere during the interim period in the future) upon which the final re-writing will be based. This Supplement is not simply a catalogue of new cases or law, but also contains any revised or altered views I may have formed since 1970, and the attempted correction of, regrettably, the many inaccuracies I have from time to time perpetrated, wherever these have come to my attention. I have also included a number of pre-1970 cases which escaped my earlier researches. In consequence, I believe that the Supplement should be of real value, when read in conjunction with the Tenth Edition, and an effective preview of the new Edition. It represents the law as at mid-1978, with apologies for the possible omission of very recent cases outside England.

It will be seen that there are far more reported cases of importance emanating from the Commonwealth and overseas than from

England, and it gives me great pleasure once again to pay tribute to what I believe to be the very high quality of their judgments. By some accident it seems that far more cases in Australia and New Zealand, for example, escape from the net of arbitration than is the case in England. There is also the almost universal tendency of the English High Court to refer building and civil engineering cases to the Official Referees, whose judgments are unfortunately rarely, if ever, reported, despite their great experience and often excellent judgments. In consequence the Commonwealth Judges appear to me on many occasions to show far more familiarity with the practices and practicalities of building and engineering contracts and projects than their English High Court brethren, on the relatively few occasions when the latter find themselves faced with a problem in this field. Given the deplorable and diffuse draftsmanship of nearly all building and civil engineering contracts throughout the world, it has become my increasingly firm belief that their proper interpretation so as to accord with the real objective intention of the parties requires, at any rate where the English rules of evidence are applied, a substantial degree of judicial knowledge of the subject-matter (as the nineteenth-century judges certainly had when they developed the law of sale of goods) to counterbalance what is often the Anglo-Saxon obsession with the literal written word, however obviously confused or anomalous it may be to the informed eye. Particularly welcome and distinguished decisions from the Commonwealth and overseas since 1970 include the judgments of the Appellate Division of South Africa in *Kathmer Investments Ltd.* v. *Woolworths* [1970] 2 S.A.L.R. 498 (where, not following the English Court of Appeal in *Crane* v. *Hegeman-Harris* [1939] 4 All E.R. 68, an arbitrator was held empowered to rectify the contract before him) and in *A. McAlpine & Son* v. *Transvaal Provincial Administration* [1974] 3 S.A.L.R. 506 (definition of reasonable time for giving information in regard to varied work, the effect of numerous variations, and of the need for notice if contract remuneration is to cease to apply); of Van Rhyn J. in *Colin* v. *De Guisti* [1975] 4 S.A.L.R. 223 (not following the English Court of Appeal in *Lynch* v. *Thorne* [1956] 1 W.L.R. 303, where a builder on whom the owner relied and who followed exactly a plan supplied to him was held liable); of Mahon J. in *Mayfield Holdings Ltd.* v. *Moana Reef Ltd.* [1973] 1 N.Z.L.R. 309 (not following Megarry J. in *Hounslow L.B.C.* v. *Twickenham Garden Developments* [1971] 2 Ch. 233 and compelling a contractor to leave the site following a purported determination of the contract by the employer) and the similar decision of Helsham J. in *Graham Roberts Ltd.* v. *Maurbeth Investments Ltd.* [1974] 1 N.S.W.L.R. 93; of Beattie J.'s application of the *Dutton* v. *Bognor Regis* case to a structural engineer at the suit of the employer in *Bevan Investments Ltd.* v. *Blackhall & Struthers* (*No.* 2) [1973] 2 N.Z.L.R. 45; of Richmond P.'s powerful judgment, on appeal in the same case in [1978] 2 N.Z.L.R. 97, on the cost of re-building as the measure of damages; of the New Zealand Court of Appeal's application of *Dutton* against a builder at the suit of a later pur-chaser in *Bowen* v. *Paramount Builders* [1977] 1 N.Z.L.R. 394 (in many ways a far clearer exposition of the new liability, and of its practical application, than the then imminent subsequent House of Lord's decision affirming *Dutton* in England of *Anns* v. *Merton Developments* [1971] 2 Ch. 233 and compelling a contractor to *L.B.C.* [1978] A.C. 728); of the High Court of Australia's interesting and clear analysis of a difficult " hybrid " re-measure-ment/lump-sum contract in *Commissioner of Roadworks* v. *Reed & Stuart Ltd.* (1974) 48 A.L.J.R. 461; and of another clear and interesting analysis of the distinction between variations and simple re-measurement, in a slightly confusing contract, by the New South Wales Court of Appeal in *Arcos Industries* v. *Electricity Commissioner of New South Wales* [1973] 2 N.S.W.L.R. 186 (it would be difficult to predict with certainty, in my view, what the English Courts would have made of either of these two last con-tracts). It follows that I am personally in entire agreement with all the above decisions. Against this (quite apart from Megarry J.'s controversial and anomalous decision in the *Hounslow* case in 1970), the English Courts in 1971 embarked on a series of six novel and, to this writer, heretical decisions in the Court of Appeal in regard to interim certificates, which caused commercial chaos in the building industry until finally over-ruled by the House of Lords in *Modern Engineering* (*Bristol*) *Ltd.* v. *Gilbert-Ash* (*Southern*) *Ltd.* [1974] A.C. 689; attempted in the Court of Appeal to decide a most interesting question on the finality of the architect's certifi-cate with regard to liquidated damages, but unfortunately did so in terms which failed to explain clearly the *ratio decidendi* or the exact consequences of the decision either in the instant case or in other more common forms of contract (*Brightside Kilpatrick Engineering Services* v. *Mitchell Construction* [1975] 2 Lloyd's Rep. 493, distinguishing, on grounds which were not clear, the

INTRODUCTION

decision of Forbes J. in *Ramac* v. *Lesser* [1975] 2 Lloyd's Rep. 430); produced (in the House of Lords) a decision on the very important R.I.B.A. final certificate clause which was (a) anomalous and difficult and (b) expressly stated to be possibly wrong, in view of arguments which the majority of the House considered had been raised too late in the proceedings (*Hosier and Dickinson* v. *Kaye* [1972] 1 W.L.R. 146); held (in the Court of Appeal) a structural engineer liable on an implied basis for the suitability of his design where no negligence had been found, by reasoning which is unclear but was stated to lay down no new principle (*Greaves* v. *Baynham Meikle* [1975] 1 W.L.R. 1095); and when making the most welcome decision to over-rule *Chambers* v. *Goldthorpe* [1901] 1 K.B. 624 and hold architects liable to their clients for negligence in issuing certificates, unfortunately did so in terms which leave it unclear whether architects whose certificates deal with disputes actually formulated before them at the time of the certificate will enjoy the old immunity (*Sutcliffe* v. *Thakrah* [1974] A.C. 727). By contrast, the only Commonwealth decisions appearing to present real difficulties of which I am aware are (a) that of the High Court of Australia in *Helicopter Sales* (*Australia*) *Limited* v. *Rotorwork Limited* (1974) 48 A.L.J.R. 390 (no implied term of quality where fastening bolt to be certified sound by third party manufacturer) and (b) that of *Brunswick Construction Limited* v. *Nowlan* (1975) 49 D.L.R. (3d) 93 (contractor liable for not warning employer of defect in architect's plans).

There is no doubt that by far the most important development in this field since 1970 has been the rapid expansion in the Anglo-Saxon countries of the law of tort, to a point where not only will all parties to a building or civil engineering project find themselves liable to third parties, such as later purchasers, for purely economic loss or damage if a " health or safety " defect is involved, but the parties may find tortious liability a powerful ally as between themselves where no contractual relationship is present (*e.g.* the builder proceeding against the architect) or even where there may also be a contractual relationship (see *Esso* v. *Mardon* [1976] Q.B. 801 and *Batty* v. *Metropolitan Property Realisations* [1978] 2 W.L.R. 500). A discussion of these important developments is to be found under pages 63–75 in this Supplement.

A new development since the Tenth Edition which I particularly welcome is the publication of a new series of Law Reports—the *Building Law Reports*, first published by The Builder Group in

INTRODUCTION

1976. From Volume 4 of those reports onwards the policy of these new reports has been to monitor and report otherwise unreported cases in England, including past cases, and also to report and explain by way of commentary the possible application or significance of some of the cases reported elsewhere. Nearly all the unreported cases referred to in Hudson are now or will become conveniently available in this series. The present Supplement, among other things, has sought to update the case references available in 1970 if a more authoritative reference has subsequently become available, and in the course of this process references to " B.L.R. " will be found in this Supplement wherever no established authoritative report is available. The " B.L.R. " reference is not at present given in places which are covered by an already established and reputable series of reports, but in the Eleventh Edition the B.L.R. reference will be given in all cases. Since the editors of Volume 4 onwards of B.L.R. are experienced practitioners in this field, the commentaries in B.L.R. (for which of course no equivalent exists in the established reports) are of special value, and subscribers to B.L.R. should in all cases check in their B.L.R. indexes against the case names in this Supplement to make sure that the case is not reported in B.L.R. as well. At present B.L.R. does not, however, cover cases outside England. Nearly all cases of any importance in England since 1970 are in B.L.R., as well as a number of earlier cases.

As in the case of other supplements by myself, this Supplement is noted against the page numbers in the parent work, *i.e.* the Tenth Edition.

I would be more than grateful if practitioners outside England were to inform me of any cases in their own jurisdictions which they think are of importance and have been missed either in the Tenth Edition or in this Supplement, since it is not always easy to keep track of reported cases in other jurisdictions, and publishing delays frequently mean that libraries may be two years in arrears with the latest reports. I would like to acknowledge the steady help over the years of Mr. Ian H. Barnett of Chatswood, New South Wales, in helping to keep me informed of current developments in the Australian and New South Wales jurisdictions, and that of Mr. M. J. O'Brien, Q.C., of the New Zealand Bar, who has recently joined my band of correspondent helpers. I would also be more than grateful if practitioners everywhere who in the course of their researches in individual cases consider that they have detected any

INTRODUCTION

inaccuracy of fact or opinion in Hudson would inform me of this—
they may take it for granted that I have no false pride in this
regard and will move with alacrity to correct mistakes, which I am
all too aware do exist in Hudson, particularly in regard to some
of the older cases, which were digested by me more than
20 years ago when I was but green in judgment. The sheer size of
the work and the pressure of other commitments also does lead to
slips and inaccuracies from time to time, the elimination of which
gives me real pleasure and satisfaction.

In regard to the illustrations of cases, it will be noted that both in
the Tenth Edition and in this Supplement these may not follow
very closely the headnote of the case as reported. My policy in
writing the text of illustrations is sometimes to achieve simplicity,
particularly for the benefit of non-legal readers, sometimes to use
only one facet, and perhaps not even one that is seriously in dispute,
as an illustration of a principle rather than as laying down the
principle, and sometimes to emphasise what I believe to be
the really significant facts of the case which may have evaded
the reporter and which may explain or affect either the decision
itself or its possible implications for the future. In other words,
apart from any actual errors, any dissimilarity between the text of
the illustration and the reported headnote of the case will not be
coincidental.

SUPPLEMENT TO TABLE OF CASES
OF MAIN WORK

SUPPLEMENT TO TEXT

CHAPTER 1 – GENERAL PRINCIPLES OF LAW

2   **Contra proferentem rule** as applied to English standard forms. It is submitted that the correct view as to this was expressed by Lord Pearson in *Tersons* v. *Stevenage Corporation* [1963] 2 Lloyd's Rep. 333 at p. 368, and is to be preferred to both Edmund Davies L.J.'s view in the *Jarvis* case and that of Harman L.J. in *Monmouth C.C.* v. *Costelloe and Kemple* (1965) 63 L.G.R. 429 at p. 434.

2–3   **" Package Deal " contracts.** A form of unilateral (N.F.B.T.E.) provenance is available in the United Kingdom, and has been commented on in the Author's *Further Building and Engineering Standard Forms* (Sweet and Maxwell 1973). A J.C.T. (R.I.B.A.) form is expected shortly.

4   **A simple contract** may also be inferred from conduct—but it is important to distinguish such conduct from *subsequent* conduct after a contract is in being, which now appears to be rejected in England even as evidence—see *Whitworth Estates* v. *Miller* [1970] A.C. 583 and *Wickman Machine Tools Sales* v. *Schuler* [1974] A.C. 235.

SECTION 2.   FORMATION OF A SIMPLE CONTRACT

5   **Estimate.** This word can, of course, also be used in a building contract to indicate the extent or value of work to be carried out under the contract. Whether the word used in this way will or will not impose a contractual obligation will depend upon the general content and construction of the contract as a whole—see, *e.g.* the cases referred to at pages 228–229 *post*, the *Lindsay Parkinson* case, *post*, page 551, and the recent case of *Cana Construction* v. *The Queen* (1973) 37 D.L.R. (3d) 418 in the Supreme Court of Canada.

11   **Acceptance.** Despite apparent acceptance, however, some contracts for work and materials may do no more than confer an option on the employer to order such work as he may choose—see the cases referred to *post*, pp. 228–229.

12 **The accepted contract**—these words are not, perhaps, sufficiently clear. The *finally executed* contract is what is intended.

Footnote 45. See now also *City of Box Hill* v. *Tauschke* [1974] V.R. 39 (Australia), *post,* p. 220.

13–16 SECTION 2 (6). **" Agreements to agree."** In the present context and discussion this expression should be understood to mean situations where the parties have not finally agreed on some or all of the terms of their contract, and should be distinguished from the express terms, commonly met in building and engineering contracts, contemplating the later execution of a formal written or sealed agreement—as to which see SECTION 2 (7) *infra,* pp. 16–17 and *post,* Chap. 3, pp. 217–223.

15 **(Illustrations).** See also

(a) *F. & G. Sykes (Wessex) Ltd.* v. *Fine Fare Ltd.* [1967] 1 Lloyd's Rep. 53 (Agreement for supply of stipulated number of day-old chicks for first year of five-year agreement, " and thereafter such other figures as may be agreed between the parties," with agreement terminable only on four years' notice and arbitration clause in general terms. *Held* arbitrator would have power to determine reasonable figures for second year and there was binding agreement);

(b) *King's Motors (Oxford) Ltd.* v. *Lax* [1970] 1 W.L.R. 426 (option for renewal of lease " at such rent as might be agreed." *Held,* no contract);

(c) *British Crane Hire* v. *Ipswich Plant Hire* [1975] Q.B. 303 (illustrated more fully *infra* in this Supplement under page 56, " usual conditions of trade " held incorporated where plaintiffs' crane bogged down in soft ground while using " navvimats " under control of defendant hirer's site agent);

(d) *Courtney & Fairbairn Ltd.* v. *Tolaini Bros.* [1975] 1 W.L.R. 297 (agreement " to negotiate fair and reasonable sum based on agreed estimates of net cost and general overheads with a 5 per cent. profit margin." *Held* no contract).

16 **Subject to contract.** See for the effect of express reference to submission of draft contracts to solicitors, *Horrobin* v. *Majestic Hotel (Cheltenham)* (1973) 227 E.G. 993; C.L.Y. (1974), No. 465, *per* Kerr J. Even in conveyancing contracts, if nothing remains to be negotiated, the words " subject to contract " may not prevent a binding contract coming into being—see *Michael Richards Properties* v. *Corporation of St. Saviour's Southwark* [1975] 3 All E.R. 416. For the general principle see also *Masters* v. *Cameron* (1954)

91 C.L.R. 353 (High Court of Australia) and also *Sturgeons* v.
Municipality of Toronto (1968) 70 D.L.R. (2d) 20 (Ontario S.C.).
So where tender documents provided that "The Council will by
notice under the hand of the Town Clerk certify its acceptance of
the . . . tender and the successful tenderer shall within four days
. . . execute the contract and/or sign the General Conditions" it
was held that an unconditional acceptance of the tender constituted
a binding contract, in a case where a contractor had carried out
£7,000 worth of work out of £36,000 and received £6,000 in
progress payments, notwithstanding failure to execute or sign the
contract or sign the Conditions: *City of Box Hill* v. *E. W.
Tauschke Property Ltd.* (1974) V.R. 39 (S.C. of Victoria).

17   Absence of consideration. See for a typical example *Brown and
Davis* v. *Galbraith* [1972] 1 W.L.R. 997, where a garage was
unable to recover from the owner for repairs carried out on the
instructions of the owner's insurers and with his approval when
the insurance company failed.

18   Footnote 73. *Gilbert* case is also reported in [1968] 2 All E.R.
248.

19   Add to second paragraph: Conversely, if the agreed sum due is
£5,000, a promise to accept £4,000 in full and final settlement will
be unenforceable in the absence of any contemplated action to his
detriment by the promisee, since there will be no consideration.

ILLUSTRATION

A judgment creditor for £2,090·19 agreed in writing not to take
"any proceedings whatever" on the judgment in consideration
of an immediate payment of £500 and the remainder by instalments "until the whole of the said sum of £2,090·19 shall have
been satisfied." After full payment under the agreement she sued
for interest. *Held* by the House of Lords, following *Pinnel's Case*
(1602) 5 Rep. 117a, she was entitled to recover: *Foakes* v. *Beer*
(1884) 9 App. Cas. 605.

See further the case of *D. & C. Builders* v. *Rees* [1966] 2
Q.B. 617 *infra*, p. 23 and *post*, Chap. 5, p. 348 and the two
Scottish cases of *Lord Doune* v. *John Dye & Son,* 1972 S.L.T.
(Sh.Ct.) 30 and *Henderson* v. *McDonald Swimming Pools,* 1972
S.L.T. (Sh.Ct.) 37, for facts of which see *infra* under p. 23 in this
Supplement.

SECTION 3. CONTRACTS UNDER SEAL

21   **Traditional recitals** as to examination of site etc. These in fact are not likely to have any legal effect unless exclusion of responsibility is directly expressed—*cf. e.g. Morrison-Knudsen International* v. *The Commonwealth* (1972) 46 A.L.J.R. 265, illustrated *infra* under p. 49, where the effect of several such provisions was effectively discounted by the High Court of Australia.

SECTION 4. VARIATION OF CONTRACTS

23   **D. & C. Case.** See also the two Scottish cases under p. 19 *supra*. (Cheque for £216 sent in response to request for £562 but saying it was total sum due *held* cashable on account only, and cashing of cheque for £98 " in final settlement " of balance of account held not to be a binding acceptance without more).

SECTION 5. VOID AND VOIDABLE CONTRACTS

26–27   **(b) Common mistake.** See *e.g. Amalgamated Investment Ltd.* v. *John Walker Ltd.* [1977] 1 W.L.R. 164, where at the date of its contract for sale, an old factory building advertised as suitable for development had, unknown to either party, been listed under section 54 of the Town and Country Planning Act 1971, reducing its value from £1,700,000 to £200,000, and the C.A. held the contract could not be avoided.

29   **Non est factum.** Where an innocent third party is involved, the plaintiff will also need to show that he has not been careless (*U.D.T.* v. *Western* [1976] Q.B. 513, *infra* under pp. 31–32, applying *Gallie* v. *Lee* [1971] A.C. 1004), but this will not apply as between the parties directly involved—see *e.g. Peterlin* v. *Allen* (1975) 49 A.L.J.R. 239 (High Court of Australia), *infra* under pp. 31–32.

31–32   **Gallie** v. **Lee** [1969] 2 Ch. 17, C.A.; affirmed by H.L. [1971] A.C. 1004. See also the *U.D.T.* case, *supra* under p. 29 (motor car purchaser signing standard form loan agreement in blank, in belief it was hire purchase agreement, held liable by C.A. to finance company advancing monies in good faith) and the *Peterlin* case *supra* under p. 29 (vendor who did not know English receiving second $50 cash six months after earlier grant of six month option for $50, and signing further option believing it to be receipt since own agent had told him to expect further $50, held by High Court of Australia not bound by second option).

32 **Rectification.** Footnote 25. *Joscleyne* case reference now [1970] 2 Q.B. 86, C.A.

33 **Rectification.** Precise formulation of rectified contract is not necessary if general sense is clear. Previous text is, it is submitted, too strict on this and not justified in principle or on authority— see *Hornibrook* case *infra*, p. 38.

35 **The election cases** (footnote 36). See now the C.A.'s view in *Riverlate Properties Ltd.* v. *Paul* [1975] Ch. 133, that the basis for these cases no longer exists in view of the modern availability of rectification in cases of unilateral mistake known to the other party.

36 **The submission** that a unilateral mistake would have to relate to an important and major element in the contract price should be deleted and regarded as withdrawn.

38 **Add further illustration** as follows:

A main contract contained a fluctuations clause, but it did not cover the same period as a then contemplated sub-contract. Both main and sub-contractor had as a fact always intended the main contract clause to operate in the sub-contract. After making certain payments on interim certificate the main contractor took the point against the sub-contractor that the sub-contract contained no fluctuations provision at all. *Held* by the High Court of Australia that the sub-contract should be rectified, the difficulty over dates being met by rectifying it in the sense that any payments received by the main contractor under the main contract provision in respect of the sub-contract work should be payable to the sub-contractor: *M. R. Hornibrook (Pty) Ltd.* v. *Eric Newham* (1971) 45 A.L.J.R. 523.

See also for an example of an error explained and discounted by evidence the incorrect " R.I.B.A." description in *Modern Buildings* v. *Limmer & Trinidad* [1975] 1 W.L.R. 1281, illustrated *infra* under p. 56 of this Supplement.

39 **The practical importance of this Act** may now be somewhat diminished in view of the rapid expansion since 1970 of the law of tort in regard to both negligent statements and other forms of negligence causing financial or economic damage—see *infra,* pp. 63 *et seq.* of this Supplement.

39–40 The speculative comments on these pages were described as useful by Lord Denning M.R. in *Howard Machine & Dredging Co.* v. *Ogden* [1978] Q.B. 574 at p. 594. They may be equally apposite in the application of the new United Kingdom Unfair Contract Terms Act 1977.

40 Footnote 48. Reference should be to Civil Code of Quebec, not Ontario.

SECTION 6. IMPLIED TERMS

49 Exclusion of liability for misrepresentation. Many of the traditional forms of wording designed to bring this about may fail in their intended effect, since such provisions will be construed strictly. The following case shows this in relation to an attempt to invoke one of the new areas of tortious liability.

ILLUSTRATION

Clause 3 (1) provided that the Contractor should be deemed to have informed himself as to the site and local conditions affecting the contract. Under Clause 04, the Contractor acknowledged that he had satisfied himself as to the nature and location of the work, " including . . . the physical conditions of the site, the structure and condition of the ground, and any failure by the Contractor to acquaint himself with the available information is not to relieve him from responsibility for estimating properly any difficulty or cost of performing the work, and the employer assumes no responsibility for any conclusions or stipulations made by the Contractor on the basis of information made available by the employer." A document entitled " Preliminary information for . . . Tenderers " expressly provided that the information was not part of the tender or contract documents and was not to be binding on either the employer or the tenderers or the contractor. The Contractor alleged breach of a duty in tort on the part of the employer to take reasonable care that the site information was accurate, and in particular that there had been failure to detect or warn him of the presence of cobbles in the clay subsoil. *Held,* by the High Court of Australia, that none of the quoted provisions was so worded as to be an effective disclaimer, if the duty of care existed and the site information was inaccurate due to negligence: *Morrison-Knudsen International* v. *The Commonwealth* (1972) 46 A.L.J.R. 265.

50 Second paragraph. See *e.g. Trollope & Colls Ltd.* v. *N.W. Metropolitan Hospital Board* [1973] 1 W.L.R. 601 where four variants were possible, in a case where the contract was silent, if a later phase of the contract was to be extended to take account of a late start due to delays on an earlier phase, and the H.L., over-ruling the C.A., accordingly refused to make any implication at all, though the resulting contract might in certain circumstances be wholly unreasonable—*per* Lord Cross of Chelsea, "I agree the contract does not express the parties' intention, but it is clear, and in view of the number of different meanings it is not possible to imply a term." See the case fully illustrated *infra* in this Supplement under p. 648.

50   Fourth paragraph. An example of this process can be seen in the implications made by the courts as to the extent of an employer's implied right to make use of an architect's plans and copyright— see the cases on this *infra* in this Supplement under p. 190.

51   Caveat emptor principle. This now no longer applies in the United Kingdom in cases where the vendor is also the builder or developer of a house and the defect involves safety or health, even though the damage is only economic, since a duty in tort will exist in such a case unaffected by the rule—see *infra* in this Supplement under p. 63.

52   Architect's authority. This paragraph relates, of course, to architects in private practice.

SECTION 7.   CUSTOM AND TRADE USAGE

55   P.C. and Provisional Sums. The view expressed here, and at pages 208 and 760, now appears to be confirmed by the High Court of Australia in *Tuta Products* v. *Hutcherson* (1972) 46 A.L.J.R. 119 illustrated in this Supplement *infra* under p. 205 (see particularly *per* Stephen J. there quoted).

56   Add illustrations:

(6) B were themselves plant-hire contractors, but on this occasion had contracted to do marsh reclamation work for an employer. They did not have a crane of their own available at the time, and hired one, together with its driver, from A, another plant-hire contractor. Condition 6 of A's conditions provided that B should be responsible for the recovery of the crane from soft ground. Condition 8 also provided that A should be indemnified by B " against all expenses in connection with or arising out of

the use of the plant." However, the conditions were not received by B until after the order had been accepted. The crane became bogged down due to the failure of A's driver to carry out B's site agent's instructions, followed by a later accident when the driver was doing what he was told. *Held* by the Court of Appeal, that there was no " course of dealing " between the parties (there had been only two transactions in the preceding year) which could be relied on; but both parties were in business as plant hirers, the machine was ordered in a great hurry, and both parties knew that it was the invariable practice to supply machinery on conditions like those used by A, which were both usual and similar to B's own conditions. Both parties were therefore entitled to conclude that the contract was for the supply of machines on the usual conditions even though not so stated. Neither condition, however, was wide enough to cover A's driver's negligence so that A could recover for the second mishap, and B for the first. (Dictum of Lord Reid in *McCutcheon* v. *David MacBrayne Ltd.* [1964] 1 W.L.R. 125 at p. 128 cited *infra* applied): *British Crane Hire* v. *Ipswich Plant Hire* [1975] Q.B. 303.

(7) An order from a main contractor to nominated sub-contractors required them " to supply . . . labour plant and machinery . . . in full accordance with the appropriate form for Nominated Sub-Contractors R.I.B.A. 1965 Edition." The R.I.B.A. was not connected with any form of nominated sub-contract, but had a 1963 Edition of a main contract. However the N.F.B.T.E. and the F.A.S.S. had issued in 1963 a form of nominated sub-contract (commonly known as " the Green Form ") headed " For use where the sub-contractor is nominated under the 1963 Edition of the R.I.B.A. form of main contract." *Held* by the Court of Appeal, that in the light of evidence that the words " the appropriate form for Nominated Sub-Contractors " would be understood in the trade as referring to " the Green Form," the words " R.I.B.A. 1965 Edition " were an added description not intended to restrict the preceding expression and could be ignored as a false and inaccurate description: *Modern Buildings* v. *Limmer & Trinidad* [1975] 1 W.L.R. 1281.

The fundamental principle in all such cases is perhaps most succinctly stated by Lord Reid in *McCutcheon* v. *David MacBrayne Ltd.* [1964] 1 W.L.R. 125 at p. 128, quoting from *Gloag on Contracts* (2nd ed. 1929), p. 7: " The judicial task is not to discover the actual intentions of each party; it is to decide what each was reasonably entitled to conclude from the attitude of the other."

SECTION 8. COLLATERAL AGREEMENTS

57-58 Last two paragraphs of Section 8. Add: However, this depends upon the view that the later agreement is reasonably intended as a replacement for the earlier agreement. Building contracts sometimes " grow " in stages as a collection of documents, and strict attention to chronology in the above sense may be unrealistic. Moreover, certain rules of evidence may over-turn conclusions based on simple chronology. Thus documents specially prepared for a specific project will usually over-ride general or standard printed documents or conditions (*Sutro* v. *Herbert Symons* [1917] 2 K.B. 348 at p. 361). Again the modern tendency of the English Court of Appeal under Lord Denning M.R. is to permit sufficiently clear oral terms to over-ride printed conditions of trading either as a matter of evidence, or as a " collateral warranty "—see *e.g. J. Evans & Son (Portsmouth) Ltd.* v. *Andrea Merzario Ltd.* [1976] 1 W.L.R. 1078 (C.A.), where an oral promise that containers would not be carried on deck was held to over-ride a printed exclusion clause, and *Mendelssohn* v. *Normand* [1970] 1 Q.B. 177, where Lord Denning M.R. said at p. 184 " The printed condition is rejected because it is repugnant to the express oral promise or representation." Furthermore, express attempts in printed documents or standard conditions to give them precedence over the parties' own documents, such as that in clause 12 (1) of the United Kingdom R.I.B.A. standard forms, have (not surprisingly having regard to the anomalies and injustice which such misguided provisions can often inflict impartially on both parties) received the strictest treatment in the courts (see *e.g. English Industrial Estates* v. *George Wimpey* (1973) 71 L.G.R. 127 (C.A.); 7 B.L.R. 126, where Lord Denning M.R. even suggested that such provisions should be disregarded altogether, though the remainder of the Court decided the case on other grounds).

SECTION 9. ESTOPPEL AND WAIVER

59 Add further illustrations:

(3) A contractor undertook to supply design drawings of the structural steel frame and roof-deck of a shopping mall for approval by the architect. By Article IX there was to be no change in the specification or other documents without the written authority of the employer. The employer's project manager verbally agreed a reduction in roof loadings to prevent an increase in cost, and drawings showing the reduced loadings were submitted and approved by the architect. *Held* by the Appellate Division of the S.C. of New Brunswick, that the employer was estopped, notwithstanding Article IX, from complaining of the reduced loadings, but approval by the architect did not affect the contractor's responsibility for compliance with the Building Code: *Acme Investments* v. *York Structural Steel* (1974) 9 N.B.R. (2d) 699.

(4) An employer accepted and occupied a building with knowledge that it contained defects, and agreed to the payment of retention moneys by bankers to the builder. *Held* there was no waiver or estoppel preventing him from suing for the defects: *Lamberts* v. *Spry* [1977] A.C.L.O. 749.

[Estoppel]. However, one form of estoppel may prevent an employer complaining of defects, *viz*: estoppel by record, or *res judicata*. It has been held in the United Kingdom that a building owner who sues and obtains judgment for defects cannot subsequently bring a second action on discovering further defects not known at the time or forming part of the earlier action— *Conquer* v. *Boot* [1928] 2 K.B. 336 (D.C.). Nevertheless, in *Purser (Hillingdon) Ltd.* v. *Jackson* [1977] Q.B. 166, *Conquer's* case was distinguished by Forbes J., on the somewhat slender ground that the rule did not apply to a subsequent arbitration, on the wording of the arbitration clause in question. *Conquer's* case appears to be based on old authority (which also exists in some United States jurisdictions) but otherwise appears to have little to commend it, and certainly no acceptable modern principle to justify it when limitation is always available to bar stale claims.

60   **Footnote 33.** Add reference to *M. R. Hornibrook (Pty) Ltd.* v. *Eric Newham* (1971) 45 A.L.J.R. 523, illustrated in this Supplement *post* under p. 220, and *supra* under p. 38.

Footnote 37. Add reference to *Watson* v. *Canada Permanent Trust Co.* (1972) 27 D.L.R. (3d) 735 (British Columbia S.C.).

SECTION 10.   LIABILITY APART FROM CONTRACT

62   **Last paragraph.** See also *Hornibrook's case* in Australia, illustrated *supra* under p. 38 and *infra* under p. 220, where the sub-contract was subject to a City Council's approval, and the Council did not know of or approve the differences between the main contractor's price and those of the sub-contractor. It was held by the High Court of Australia that, even if the condition of approval was effectively suspensory and had not been waived, the plaintiff, since the sub-contract had been fully executed, could recover on an implied contract or *quantum meruit*, his bargain being evidence of a reasonable price as in *Way* v. *Latilla* [1937] 3 All E.R. 759. (In *Way* v. *Latilla* the House of Lords held that where an arrangement for the introduction of business by an agent did not amount to a binding contract, due to the uncertainty of the terms as to the agent's remuneration, what had been said during negotiation could be treated as some evidence of what would be reasonable remuneration on an implied promise to pay in a case where services had in fact been performed).

63–75 **There have been major extensions in the law of tort** since 1970 particularly affecting building and civil engineering contracts. These extensions have occurred in three principal areas.

The first area of novelty, common to the other two, is that liability in tort is now being imposed where *only* economic or financial loss, as opposed to physical damage to person or property, has been suffered by the plaintiff. At the time of writing the Tenth Edition, such claims appeared to be limited in England to cases where the new principle in *Hedley-Byrne* v. *Heller*, imposing liability for negligent misrepresentation in certain special circumstances, could be applied. It is now clear that all parties concerned with a work of building or civil engineering will, if the element of health or safety is involved and they have been negligent, be liable for the purely financial loss suffered by a subsequent owner of the property in remedying any such defects when discovered by him. Nor will the rule of *caveat emptor* protect a negligent vendor from such an action if he was the builder or developer. The possibility of the law moving in this direction was in fact discussed in the Tenth Edition at p. 81.

The second area of novelty arises because the new liability for construction is in a special sense wider than that of " product liability " in the United States, for example, or of dangerous chattels in the United Kingdom, since the liability is, by analogy, for the repair *of the chattel or product itself*, not of the damage done by it (see *e.g. Trans World Airlines Inc.* v. *Curtiss Wright Corp.* (1955) 148 N.Y.S. (2d) 284 for the traditional view of this distinction). The United Kingdom authorities for all the above propositions commence with the Court of Appeal decision in *Dutton* v. *Bognor Regis U.D.C.* [1972] 1 Q.B. 373 (illustrated *infra* in this Supplement under p. 81), which was widely regarded as revolutionary, but was effectively confirmed and approved by the House of Lords in *Anns* v. *Merton L.B.C.* [1978] A.C. 728. In both cases the local authority was held liable for the negligence of its building inspector to subsequent purchasers of houses containing defects and requiring repair. For the full implications of these

65-75 decisions see the author's two Notes and Article in (1977) 93
(cont.) L.Q.R. 16, (1978) 94 L.Q.R. 60, and (1978) 94 L.Q.R. 331 (this
latter a Note on the *Batty* case, infra). Though these two English
cases are specifically concerned with local authority inspectors
as defendants, they clearly apply to all other persons concerned
with the production of buildings or structures. The *Dutton* case was
rapidly so applied throughout the Commonwealth, and in *Batty*
v. *Metropolitan Property Realisations* [1978] Q.B. 554 (illustrated
infra in this Supplement under p. 81) the Court of Appeal in
England had no difficulty in extending the liability against
both builder and developer in favour of a later purchaser. This
latter case, incidentally, goes far to show that no physical damage is
necessary to establish liability (see also dissenting judgments in
the Supreme Court of Canada of Laskin and Hall JJ. in *Rivtow
Marine Ltd.* v. *Washington Iron Works* (1973) 6 W.W.R. 692 and
the unanimous (though *obiter*) views of the New Zealand Court of
Appeal in *Bowen* v. *Paramount Builders* [1977] 1 N.Z.L.R. 394).
In the *Bowen* case (illustrated in this Supplement under p. 81) it
was a builder who was held liable in tort to a later purchaser, but in
Brook Enterprises v. *Welding* (1973) 38 D.L.R. (3d) 472 the British
Columbia S.C. held a vendor's architect liable to a subsequent
purchaser of a motel, following *Dutton*, and in *Bevan Investments*
v. *Blackhall and Struthers* (*No.* 2) [1973] 2 N.Z.L.R. 45 (illustrated
in this Supplement under p. 81) the New Zealand S.C. held a
consulting engineer, called in privately by an architect to design the
structure of a sports centre, liable to the owner in tort, again
following *Dutton* (see also this case affirmed at a much later date in
[1978] 2 N.Z.L.R. 97). Again, in *District of Surrey* v. *Church*
(1977) 76 D.L.R. (3d) 721 the British Columbia S.C. similarly held
that a consulting engineer, who had advised his architect client to
have a deep soil survey carried out, but when none was, took no
steps to warn the owner, was liable to the building owner in tort
(see the case illustrated *infra* in this Supplement under p. 133).

Not only has the rule in *Otto* v. *Bolton* (*caveat emptor*) now been
formally abrogated by the House of Lords, but it is clear that the
new tortious liability can exist independently of any co-existent
liability of the defendant to the plaintiff in contract—see *Esso* v.
Mardon [1976] Q.B. 801, and *Batty* v. *Metropolitan Property
Realisations, supra*. The new liability has, with the United Kingdom
Limitation Acts basing the start of the period on the date of the
cause of action arising, posed formidable problems of analysis

63–75
(cont.) from this point of view, and the United Kingdom litigation has in fact been principally concerned with this aspect, and with certain *obiter dicta* on this in *Dutton's* case, which were widely followed in the United Kingdom and elsewhere (see *e.g. Brook Enterprises* v. *Welding* (1973) 38 D.L.R. (3d) 472, where, on a similar statutory basis of limitation, a purchaser's cause of action was held by the British Columbia S.C. to arise at the date of his acquisition of the property). However, in the *Anns* case the House of Lords held that this new cause of action arises when " the state of the building is such that there is present or imminent danger to the health or safety of persons occupying it." The present author has suggested that there may be practical and analytical difficulties which will require modification of this last formulation, particularly in cases where no physical damage has as yet occurred—see (1978) 94 L.Q.R. at p. 68, and the reference to a possible modification of Lord Denning M.R.'s rather different formulation in the Court of Appeal in *Sparham-Souter* v. *Town and Country Developments* [1976] Q.B. 858. Moreover, it is clear that in this type of case there is a real possibility of successive instances of physical damage—see the judgments of the New Zealand Court of Appeal in the *Paramount Building* case, *supra*, which represent in many ways, and particularly from the point of view of practitioners, much the most clear and thorough examination of the whole topic in any jurisdiction.

So far as the *quantum* of damage is concerned, while this new liability will usually involve cost of repair, diminution in value of the construction may be obtained in appropriate cases—see *Bowen* v. *Paramount Builders, supra* and *Batty's* case, *supra*—while loss of earnings from commercial buildings during repairs will be recoverable—see the *Bevan Investments* case, *supra*. For a review of some of the United States authorities, where the same tortious liability of vendors and builders appears to have emerged a decade earlier, see (1978) 94 L.Q.R. 70–72. In some United States jurisdictions the liability appears to extend beyond strictly safety aspects to what are amenity or business aspects, (see *Pollard* v. *Saxe* (1974) 88P. (2d) 525), but there is no sign of this in England or the Commonwealth as yet—see *e.g. Sealand of Pacific* v. *McHaffie* (1974) 51 D.L.R. (3d) 702, where the British Columbia Court of Appeal appear to have rejected tortious liability asserted against a partner of a firm of naval architects, which had been found liable in contract, on the ground that safety considerations were not involved. For a wide review of the new liability, see also Cane in (1979) 95 L.Q.R. 117.

The third principal area of extension of liability in tort affecting building and civil engineering contracts is in the field of negligent misrepresentation and the *Hedley Byrne* v. *Heller* principle of liability. In the case of *Ministry of Housing etc.* v. *Sharp* [1970] 2 Q.B. 223 a negligent statement was made to a purchaser of land by the public servant responsible for the upkeep of a local land charges register. Far from damaging the representee, it positively benefited him, but third persons having certain charges on the land lost their right to enforce them, and one of them, in fact the Minister, was held entitled to recover his financial loss—see *per* Salmon L.J. " The present case does not fit into any category of negligence yet considered by the Courts. The plaintiff has not been misled by any careless statement made to him or to someone else who would be likely to pass it on to a third person such as the plaintiff, as in *Hedley Byrne* v. *Heller*." Even without the benefit of *Sharp's* case, it is clear that designers, consultants carrying out surveys or making reports, and employers making representations as to the site, will all be in the category of possible defendants at the suit of third parties not in direct contractual relations with them, and while this liability has existed for many years where physical damage to person or property resulted, its extension to cases where the loss is anticipated or economic only is potentially extremely important. Prior to *Hedley Byrne* very occasional cases of such liability occurred—see for example the well-known United States cases of *Glanzer* v. *Shepard* (1922) 233 N.Y. 236 (where such a liability was upheld) and *Ultramares* v. *Touche* (1931) 253 N.Y. 170 (where it was refused). A remarkable review of the authorities on negligent misrepresentation, including *Hedley Byrne*, is to be found in the judgment of the Supreme Court of Illinois in *Rozny* v. *Marnul* (1969) 250 N.E. (2d) 656, where a land surveyor was held liable in tort for economic loss to a later purchaser of an inaccurately surveyed and recorded building plot. But the modern tendency, exemplified in England in *Sharp's* case, undoubtedly seems to be to blur the distinction, in economic loss cases, between a misrepresentation made to a particular person, and a general duty of care owed to a wider class of persons. Not surprisingly, contractors, who will suffer a special kind of economic loss if a design or survey is negligent, have sought to invoke tortious liability to recover their loss. In *Miller* v. *Dames and Moore* [1961] Cal.App.

65–75 (2d) 305 a Californian Court of Appeal held a firm of soil engineers
(cont.) employed by a local authority's consulting engineers liable in tort
to contractors for an outfall sewer system, for economic loss
(reduced profitability) which resulted from a negligent soils survey
carried out prior to tenders being invited, in the absence of
evidence that the defendants did not know that their report was
intended to provide information to tenderers, and even though the
contract documents contained express exclusions of liability pro-
tecting the authority and their consulting engineers, though not
the soils engineers. (This case was cited by Dean Prosser in his
article Misrepresentation and Third Persons in (1966) 19 Vanderbilt
L.R. 231 and by the Supreme Court of Illinois in 1969 in the *Rozny*
case). On the other hand, in *Vermont Construction* v. *Beatson*
(1976) 67 D.L.R. (3d) 95 a contractor sued an architect for
economic loss, on the ground that defects in his plans affecting the
stability of the work during construction made the performance of
the contract less profitable, but the Supreme Court of Canada
rejected liability as a matter of law. (It is not, however, entirely
clear from the report how far this decision was based on the civil
law of Quebec and certain special provisions of Quebec law
relating to a builder's joint responsibility for design with the architect). See also for a careful statement of the extent of such a
possible duty in England, the judgment of H.H. Judge Stabb Q.C.,
in *Oldschool* v. *Gleesons* (1976) 4 B.L.R. 103 at pp. 130–132.
Earlier the High Court of Australia, in a case where contractors
brought an action in tort for failing to take reasonable care that the
site information was accurate, in that large quantities of cobbles in
the underlying clays were not disclosed, expressed no opinion as to
the likely chances of success, as a matter of law, of the principal
claim, while rejecting a number of defences based upon alleged
exclusion clauses in the contract—see *Morrison-Knudsen International* v. *The Commonwealth* (1972) 46 A.L.J.R. 265, illustrated
supra in this Supplement under p. 49. As a final comment on this
last area of extension of the law of tort it may perhaps be stated
that the early Californian *Miller* case, *supra*, does seem consistent
with the principle of the later Court of Appeal judgments in
England in the *Hedley Byrne* and *Sharp* cases, *supra*, subject, however, to any tendency the English courts may develop, as fore-
shadowed in the *Anns* case, to limit economic loss liability in tort in
the construction field to questions of safety or health if no
misrepresentation is involved. No case involving a contractor's

economic loss has yet reached the Courts in England, but the House of Lords decisions in *Sutcliffe* v. *Thakrah* and *Arenson* v. *Casson Beckman*, rejecting an alleged immunity from suit of certifiers, may be expected to lead rapidly to actions *by contractors* in tort for carelessness in certifying—see *infra* under pp. 165–9. Finally, attention must be drawn to the Defective Premises Act 1972 which, in the case of dwelling-houses at least, the *Dutton* case appeared substantially to anticipate. The Act, of course, has a fixed period of limitation, and may be largely circumvented in the case of houses constructed under approved schemes under the Act. It will be the subject of more detailed comment in the next Edition.

64 **Hedley Byrne v. Heller.** The two House of Lords decisions in *Sutcliffe* v. *Thakrah* and *Arenson* v. *Casson Beckman*, which remove the immunity hitherto thought to be enjoyed by certifiers (see the discussion *infra* in this Supplement under pp. 165–169), are of great importance in the context of the present field of liability, since it would seem that, at least where no dispute has been formulated, *contractors* will be able to sue certifiers in tort for carelessness in issuing their certificates—see *supra* in this supplement under pp. 63–75 and *infra* under pp. 165–9 and, in particular, the important judgment of the S.C. of Illinois in *Rozny* v. *Marnul* (1969) 250 N.E. (2d) 656 there referred to. See, for the expansion of this area of liability, the discussion *supra* under pp. 63–75.

68 **Contribution for joint tort.** See now the new right of contribution in England, available to or against a person liable in contract as well as tort in respect of the same damage, under the Civil Liability (Contribution) Act 1978, commented on shortly *infra* in this Supplement under pp. 306–310.

69–71 **Architect's duty to Contractor** in regard to method of working and design—see also the Canadian S.C. case of *City of Prince Albert* v. *Underwood McLellan*, illustrated and commented on under p. 153 *infra*.

73 **Illustration (5).** *Clayton* v. *Woodman*. It should perhaps be added that the contract provided expressly that the Contractor should carry out and complete the works " in accordance with this contract and in every respect in accordance with the directions . . . of the architect."

74   **Illustration (6).** *Voli's* case. Reference should be to the High Court of Australia, not Queensland, and footnote reference should be 110 C.L.R. 74.

78   **Contribution for joint tort.** See now the new right of contribution in England, available to or against a person liable in contract as well as tort in respect of the same damage, under the Civil Liability (Contribution) Act 1978, commented on shortly *infra* in this Supplement under pp. 306–310.

81   **These speculative and in part prophetic comments** now require to be read in the light of the discussion *supra* in this Supplement under pp. 63–75. In (1978) 94 L.Q.R. at p. 68 the author has suggested that the *Anns* case in England must logically apply to plant, machinery or goods, if health or safety considerations are involved. See also Cane in (1979) 95 L.Q.R. 117. If this is correct, it will afford employers a remedy against suppliers or sub-contractors, at least where the health or safety factor is present, despite the absence of contractual relations.

Chapter 1, Section 10. Defective Premises Act 1972. In the next edition an additional sub-section will be included dealing shortly with this Act.

82   **Development of law of tort.** As already indicated in the discussion *supra* in this Supplement under pp. 65–73, the law of tort has expanded rapidly in the directions contemplated and indeed welcomed on this page in the Tenth Edition. The following cases, commented on in the discussion *supra*, are illustrated here as practical examples of the new liability. In addition to the cases here illustrated, see also the Canadian case of *District of Surrey* v. *Church*, illustrated *infra* in this Supplement under p. 133, and the other cases referred to in the discussion *supra* under pp. 63–73.

ILLUSTRATIONS

(1) A local authority failed to appreciate that a private developer's building was being constructed on " made ground," and their building inspector passed trenches and foundations which a careful inspection would have shown to be insufficient to deal with this condition. After the house was built it passed through two sets of hands, the second purchaser not employing a surveyor, though her mortgagees had done so. The house subsequently settled and developed cracks which required repair. *Held* by the Court of Appeal, the Council's servants owed a duty

of care in tort to the second purchaser, and the duty extended to economic loss: *Dutton* v. *Bognor Regis U.D.C.* [1972] 1 Q.B. 373.

[*Note:* For very similar facts (defect a failure to take foundations down to depths shown on drawings) see *Anns* v. *Merton L.B.C.* [1978] A.C. 728.]

(2) An architect employed a consulting engineer for the design and supervision of the structural part of a sports centre. The building owner entered into a contract using this design. The contractor eventually stopped work as the design, which departed from the relevant engineering codes, was found to be unsafe, and it was necessary to change the plans and incur additional expense. The owner sued for the cost of reinstatement to a proper standard, and loss of profit due to the delay. *Held* by the S.C. of New Zealand (Beattie J.), that the architect was liable to the owner in contract and the engineer in tort: *Bevan Investments Ltd.* v. *Blackhall & Struthers* [1973] 2 N.Z.L.R. 45.

[*Note:* This case has been affirmed at all points by the New Zealand C.A. in [1978] 2 N.Z.L.R. 97.]

(3) Vendors of land in known peat country promised to provide an adequate " sandpad " on it. There was little experience of building on such land available at the time. The purchaser, who intended to use the land for a building investment, gave a rough floor plan, showing two flats, to his builders. The builders inquired and were assured both by the vendors and the purchaser client that adequate steps had been taken to enable normal foundations to be used, and designed accordingly, though the contract entitled the builder to extra payment if additional footings due to the peat were required. Subsequently the building inspector stopped the work as he was dissatisfied with the adequacy of a " sandpad " sub-foundation for a peat area. The builders then wrote to the building inspectorate substituting concrete floors with footings to rest on a 12″ sandfill raft (a normal specification for a concrete floor on normal foundations) but with no change of the sub-foundations. No reply was received and the builders re-started work. The inspector subsequently visited and said nothing. After noting certain signs of misalignment in the main brick wall, and after certain work concealing this was done by the builders, the purchaser, who had become uneasy about the building, sold the building when it was nearly complete to a second purchaser without any warning. Shortly after, a major subsidence took place. *Held* by the Court of Appeal of New Zealand, that on the facts the builders should have at least obtained the explicit approval of the inspectorate and of their own client, whom they should have warned of the inspectorate's doubts and of their own lack of experience, and the builders were accordingly liable in tort to the second purchaser for the reasonable cost of repair, together with a sum representing a permanent diminution in the market value of the building: *Bowen* v. *Paramount Builders* [1977] 1 N.Z.L.R. 394.

[*Note:* The judgments in this case are discussed in greater detail in the author's Note in (1978) 94 L.Q.R. at pp. 69–70.]

(4) A developer and builder walked over an area subject to landslip, and as a result of their inspection decided to go ahead

with a development, the builder purchasing the land and selling it to the developer, who then financed the construction of the houses upon it by the builder. Nothing on the land itself indicated that anything might be wrong, but suspicious signs did exist on land nearby and on adjoining land. A serious slip occurred on land below one of the houses after it had been sold, which damaged the house's garden but not the house itself or its foundations. However, the evidence was that the house was now eventually doomed, since within 10 years further movement was inevitable which would ultimately destroy the foundations. The purchaser sued the developer in contract and tort, and the builder in tort only. *Held* by the Court of Appeal, following *Esso Petroleum* v. *Mardon* [1976] Q.B. 801, that the developer might be liable in tort as well as in contract, and, following *Anns* v. *Merton L.B.C.*, that both developer and builder were liable in tort. Since the house was undamaged, but unsaleable and virtually valueless, the measure of damage was the loss of value, plus a small sum of damages for the second plaintiff (the wife of the first plaintiff) for physical and mental distress: *Batty* v. *Metropolitan Property Realisations Ltd.* [1978] Q.B. 554.

CHAPTER 2 – ARCHITECTS, ENGINEERS AND SURVEYORS

SECTION 2. DEFINITIONS AND QUALIFICATIONS

90 **First paragraph.** In addition many modern engineering designs may, while not actually dictating the methods of construction, be based on assumptions that come close to this—*e.g.* box-girder bridges.

Second paragraph. Perhaps the most important special class, now amounting to a separate profession, are structural engineers, who are almost invariably used on any substantial building project to design the framework and structure, and if necessary to supervise their construction, as well as on civil engineering projects. Many architects' firms employ such engineers or have them as partners— see SECTION 2 (6), pp. 97–98 *infra*. A further specialisation of increasing importance is the soils engineer, specialising in the relatively new field of soils mechanics, who in cases of doubtful ground or geology may be called in to organise and carry out pre-contract surveys and provide reports and recommendations in regard to ground conditions and the design of foundations and associated temporary or permanent works—a typical example of this relationship is to be found in the facts of the 1961 Californian case of *Miller* v. *Dames and Moore*, *supra* in this Supplement under pp. 63–75, and of negligence in failing to advise such a survey in the 1977 British Columbian case of *District of Surrey* v. *Church* also referred to *supra* under pp. 63–75, and illustrated *infra* under p. 133.

SECTION 3. CONTRACT OF EMPLOYMENT

99 **Incorporation of R.I.B.A. Conditions of Engagement** including arbitration clause. See *Kaye* v. *Bronesky,* 4 B.L.R. 4 (C.A.).

103 **Add to paragraph (2):**
or to make arrangements for such an examination, including advising on the need for the employment of specialists or consultants.
Add to paragraph (5):
including advising on the need for the employment of any specialists or consultants.

SECTION 4. AUTHORITY OF THE ARCHITECT AND ENGINEER

107 **In the latest (Fifth Edition) I.C.E. Conditions** all finality has been removed in regard to the Maintenance Certificate, and no finality attaches to the new Final Certificate under that contract. The R.I.B.A. forms have also been amended in such a way as to remove nearly all finality from the final certificate.

108 **Architect's authority under express power to vary.** Even in this case, United Kingdom contracts do not at the present day attach any finality, should either party wish to dispute it, to the architect's opinion order or decision as to a variation.

110 **First paragraph.** Second line should read "may be held to have ratified . . . "

SECTION 6. DUTIES AND LIABILITIES OF ARCHITECTS AND ENGINEERS TO EMPLOYER

123 **Section 6 (1).** This section requires considerable revision in the light of the new expanded liability of architects and engineers in economic loss cases, discussed in detail *supra* in this Supplement under pp. 63–75. There seems little doubt that *Bagot* v. *Stevens Scanlan* must be treated as overruled—see *per* Lord Denning M.R. in *Esso* v. *Mardon* (1976) Q.B. 801 at pp. 818–820, and *per* Megaw

L.J. in *Batty* v. *Metropolitan Realisations* [1978] Q.B. 554 at p. 566. In consequence, an architect will now be liable in tort to his client if he comes within the *Hedley Byrne* principle as extended in 1970 in *Sharp's* case, or under the special "safety or health" principle in *Dutton's* case and *Anns'* case, or any other recognised field of tortious negligence.

For the application of limitation of action under English law, particularly in the *Dutton* and *Anns* economic loss cases, see also the discussion in this Supplement under pp. 63–75, and the doubts there expressed as to the *Anns* formulation of the time when the cause of action arises. The rule of limitation *in contract* is reasonably clear—see *e.g. White* v. *Taupo Totara* (1960) N.Z.L.R. 547. See also the English leading cases of *Cartledge* v. *Jopling* [1963] 1 All E.R. 341 and *Letang* v. *Cooper* [1964] 2 All E.R. 929 on the irrelevance of the practical "undiscoverability" of a cause of action if no fraudulent concealment is present, but the different view now apparently taken in the economic loss cases.

It should, however, be borne in mind that the professional duty of an architect is likely to be a continuing one during his relationship with his client, so that it will often be possible to show a late date for the last possible breach on which to found the action— "I think where act or omission . . . is not something of a final or irreparable nature a professional man is under a continuing duty to his client during the subsistence of the professional relationship to make good, at his own expense if need be, any defects which occur as a result of his breach of duty. In the present case the relationship continued until . . . his final certificate," ". . . we think that, generally speaking, a professional man is engaged to 'see the business through' . . . in the present case . . . the defendant's employment and engagement were in the nature of an entire contract, namely to design the house, let the contract, supervise the buildings, and advise the plaintiff with respect to payment of the builder and acceptance of the work," *per* Napier L.C.J. in the Full Court of South Australia in *Edelman* v. *Boehm* (May 1, 1964, S.A. Law Society Judgment Notices).

It is submitted that in these cases the breach will continue at least until such time as it would cease to be practicable to order a variation or otherwise cure the defect or remedy the breach.

124– The classical definition now appears to be that formulated by
125 McNair J. in *Bolam* v. *Friern Hospital* [1957] 1 W.L.R. 582 at

p. 586 (a medical case) as subsequently approved by the Privy Council in *Chin Keow* v. *Government of Malaysia* [1967] 1 W.L.R. 813, *viz.*: " it is sufficient if he exercises the ordinary skill of an ordinary competent man exercising that particular act." (This should not be read, it is submitted, as in any way down-grading the responsibility of persons offering a specialised or unusual service, or choosing to employ a new technique, or as a fact enjoying some special knowledge which is not generally available.)

A warning should perhaps be given that the discussion at pp. 124–126 is concerned with those areas of responsibility where an element of professional judgment or opinion or competence is involved. Architects and engineers frequently operate as large firms, offering what is in effect a comprehensive service, with sometimes a degree of sub-contracting (*e.g.* for the sinking of exploratory boreholes or the provision of laboratory or geological services) or of sub-consultation in other fields in cases where sufficiently qualified staff or partners are not available. In such cases they will be liable, it is submitted, if mistakes or incompetence occur in delegated work or services, or for simple administrative errors of their own staff, even if no element of professional negligence or personal blame is to be attached to the partners or their qualified staff. In such areas, particularly since judgment is not involved, their obligation may, on the analogy of sale of goods, be to provide a service which is suitable for the purpose for which it is required (compare the responsibility of solicitors for the administrative errors of their employees). However, in a most difficult case the English Court of Appeal appears to have come perilously close to this position even where professional competence was directly in issue.

ILLUSTRATION

A package-deal (or " turn-key ") contractor engaged structural engineers to design the frame of the building, the floors of which had to take the weight of stacker trucks moving over the floors carrying oil drums. The floors as designed had not sufficient strength to withstand the resonance forces set up by the moving trucks. The trial judge expressly held that there was no negligence but implied a term of suitability, alternatively suggesting that in the case of structural engineers a higher duty might be implied by law than that generally owed by professional men. *Held* by the Court of Appeal, the defendants were liable on an implied warranty of suitability arising from the particular facts (not by law) due to the Contractor's engagement of the engineer to design a suitable floor; alternatively, despite his stated conclusion, the trial judge had in reality found negligence as a fact.

However, no higher duty rested on a structural engineer than that formulated in *Bolam's* case for professional men generally: *Greaves* v. *Baynham Meikle* [1975] 1 W.L.R. 1095.

[*Note*: There are obvious difficulties in following the precise logic of this case. The evidence cited by the Court in support of the implied term appears to show no more than that the contractor client made known to his engineer the purpose for which the floors were required. The contractor himself was, of course, liable, in the absence of exclusion in his own contract, for a suitable building independent of any fault on his part. None of these facts seems, on consideration, sufficient to support such an implied term in English law. On the other hand, the trial judge did appear to attach undue weight to a possible literal interpretation of the relevant United Kingdom Code of Practice for concrete floors when stating that there had been no negligence, and there is therefore something to be said for the second ground on which the Court based its decision. It seems quite clear, on any view, that the case lays down no general principle.]

125– **R.I.B.A. final certificate.** This finality has now at last been largely
126 removed from the forms by amended wording—see the comment under p. 107 *supra,* and the new wording and discussion *post* in this Supplement under p. 490. The I.C.E. forms no longer have finality either—see under p. 107, *supra.*

127 **Add second illustration:**

Naval architects were employed for the reconstruction of an oceanarium. Prior to their being employed, the owners had received representations from the suppliers of a product (vermiculite concrete) that it would be suitable for a special underwater use. The suppliers made the same representations to the architects. *Held* by the Court of Appeal of British Columbia, on the facts the architects owed a duty to make further inquiries, and they as well as the suppliers were liable to the owners: *Sealand of the Pacific* v. *Robert McHaffie Ltd.* (1974) 51 D.L.R. (3d) 702.

128 **Add to Footnote 31:** See for an exact example of this the case of *District of Surrey* v. *Church* (1977) 76 D.L.R. (3d) 721 (British Columbia S.C.) illustrated *infra* in this Supplement under p. 133.

133 **Illustration (1)** (*Moneypenny's* case). Strike out last sentence and substitute:

" Bovill C.J. directed the jury that on these facts the engineer would not be entitled to his remuneration."

Add further illustration:

(3) An architect employed to design a police station engaged consulting structural engineers, who were not specialist soil engineers, to examine shallow test-pits on the site. The consultants twice suggested a deeper soil investigation, having seen silty clays, but were told by the architect that the owners would

CHAPTER 2 – ARCHITECTS, ENGINEERS AND SURVEYORS

not authorise this. This was not in fact true. The consultants then prepared a foundation and structural design based on their visual estimate of the bearing capacity of the material in the test-pits. Later the building inspector asked for a soils report before giving a building permit and, in response to pressure from the architect, the consultants sent a letter stating what they had seen in the pits, and that the material had a substantial bearing capacity. The published geology of the site showed the subsoil for between 100 and 150 feet consisted of soft compressible marine clays. Differential settlement ultimately took place. *Held* by the British Columbia S.C. (Munroe J.) that the architect, who knew that the consultants were not soil specialists, was liable in contract for failing to obtain a deep soil survey as recommended by the consultants, and that the consultants, who knew that the owners would rely on their skill and judgment and did not know of their limited experience in soil mechanics, were liable to them in tort. In the circumstances notice to the architect as the owner's agent of the need for a further survey was not a sufficient discharge of their duty, and they should have made certain that knowledge of their recommendation reached the owners: *District of Surrey* v. *Church* (1977) 76 D.L.R. (3d) 721.

136 Criterion (a). In general the employer will not be obliged to furnish information or possession earlier than would otherwise be the case merely by reason of progress ahead of any programme or the contract period, it is submitted. See also for the abuse of contractual provisions requiring the contractor to supply a post-contract programme, Chapter 9, p. 603.

137 Add further illustration:

A contractor for a motorway using a traditional I.C.E.-style contract pleaded three alternative formulations of the time for supplying information and giving instructions with regard to variations *viz.*: (a) at a reasonable time (which he contended meant a time convenient and profitable to himself), or (b) at a time so as not to cause inconvenience loss or expense, or (c) so that the works could be arranged and executed efficiently and economically. The Court were asked for declaratory relief defining the implied term. *Held* by the Appellate Division of the Supreme Court of South Africa (a) by a majority, that the Contractor was not entitled to declaratory relief in specific terms; (b) that under this type of contract valid variations might be ordered at any time and irrespective of the stage of progress of the work. *Per* Corbett A.J.A., that the employer was obliged to issue such drawings or give such instructions as might be reasonably required by the Contractor in order to enable him to execute the works as defined in the general conditions. Each such drawing and instructions should be issued or given, as the case might be, within a reasonable time after the obligation arose. This formulation covered both contract and varied work, and related only to the instructions without which the Contractor could not proceed. It had no application to the variation order itself. *Per* Jansen J.A., agreeing with Corbett A.J.A., the duty in regard to contract work (*i.e.* further necessary drawings) would arise when it was known that a particular drawing or instruction was required. The same duty might also arise following the issue of a variation instruction, but the time for giving the variation instruction itself is not governed by this principle and should be distinguished: *A. MacAlpine & Son* v. *Transvaal Provincial Administration* [1974] 3 S.A.L.R. 506.

[*Note*: Corbett A.J.A.'s judgment, which refers to the same criteria as those set out at p. 136 of the Tenth Edition, as further emphasised by Jansen J.A., appears to make an entirely correct, and the clearest available analysis to date, of this implied term. The majority appear to have preferred not to go beyond a simple "reasonable time" formulation, but there is every indication in the other judgments of agreement with the formulation of Corbett A.J.A. as further explained by Jansen J.A.]

140 **The Kingston-upon-Hull case.** See for the contract provisions p. 388 of the Tenth Edition. Its principle appears to have been lost sight of to some extent in *City of Prince Albert* v. *Underwood McLellan* (1969), illustrated *infra* in this Supplement under p. 153.

148 **Footnote 87a.** The *Gleeson* appeal was not ultimately proceeded with. See, however, the attitude of Lord Denning M.R. to the same provision in *English Industrial Estates* v. *George Wimpey*, referred to *supra* in this Supplement under pp. 57–58.

Supervision. One consequence of an architect being employed to supervise the builder may be that a continuing duty will persist until completion in regard to other duties previously performed by him—*e.g.* the design of the work—so that a later cause of action can, for purposes of limitation, be pleaded, on the basis, for example, that an original design error or defective work could have been detected and corrected at a later stage during the construction period—see the unreported South Australian case of *Edelman* v. *Boehm* referred to in this Supplement *supra* under p. 123.

152 **R.I.B.A. final certificate clause.** This has at last been amended and the certificate will in the great majority of cases have no finality—see *infra* in this Supplement under p. 490.

152–
153 **Same damage for different defendants.** Only if the damages are "realised" against one defendant will the other be afforded a defence—see *e.g. Campbell Flour Mills* v. *Bowes & Ellis* (1914)

32 O.L.R. 270, where an employer was given judgment against both architects and contractors for defective materials, and a defence that he must elect between the two was rejected; and see as a further factual example *Sealand of the Pacific* v. *Robert McHaffie,* illustrated *supra* in this Supplement under p. 127. See also the ingenious scheme in *City of Prince Albert* v. *Underwood McLellan* illustrated under p. 153 *infra,* whereby a defendant contractor's sureties paid the plaintiff in full in return for subrogation to the plaintiff's rights against his engineer, which surprisingly succeeded in the Supreme Court of Canada. It has been a lacuna in English law that there is no right of contribution in such cases, except in the case of joint tortfeasors, but see now the Civil Liability (Contribution) Act 1978, commented on shortly *infra* in this Supplement under pp. 306–310.

153 Add second illustration:

Engineers designed a dam with a pre-stressed concrete circular structure requiring careful backfilling with earth in layers round the perimeter due to its exceptional lightness. The engineers were to supervise the construction " including resident supervision for continuous daily inspection and guidance of the contractor." There were other powers of general supervision and direction, and to stop progress in order to ensure proper execution of the work. The backfill was to be deposited in layers and carefully consolidated " to lines and grades indicated on the drawings as indicated by the engineer." On completion before backfilling, tests showed leaks on 30 per cent. of the perimeter, which prevented backfilling this part for the time being. The engineer told the contractor not to backfill the remainder beyond 10ft. from the bottom, but by the next day the contractor had backfilled the 70 per cent. watertight part up to 24ft. The engineer asked him why, but ended the discussion with the words, " It is up to you Bill." The dam collapsed due to the extent of this differential backfilling, and the contractor refused to continue working when ordered to re-execute except on a " without prejudice " basis. He was dismissed and the work completed by another contractor. Under a complicated arrangement the contractor's sureties paid the owner his losses in full in return for being subrogated to the owner's rights against the engineer. The trial judge held that the engineer's failure to supervise the backfilling properly was the " prime cause " of the collapse and then expressed the view that the contractor was justified in taking the stand which he did, but he and the Court of Appeal both considered that the owners had suffered no damage, having been paid in full. *Held* by the Supreme Court of Canada (Cartwright C.J.C. and Spence J. dissenting) that since the employer would be bound to hand over the proceeds of the action to the sureties if successful, there would not be a double recovery, and the owner could succeed: *City of Prince Albert* v. *Underwood McLellan* (1969) 3 D.L.R. (3d) 385.

[*Note*: It is difficult to accept the majority reasoning on the "double damage" point in this case—the owner was indemnified in every way, and would not have had to hand back the sureties' payment if the action was lost. Leaving this aside, it is clear that the attention of the trial judge was primarily on the "no damage" defence, but his views as to the "prime cause" of the failure, which was due to straightforward breach of contract by the contractor, seem impossible to justify, and were obviously not shared by the higher tribunals. It is submitted that the engineer's powers were in the nature of an option to be exercised on behalf of the employer in the interest of the final permanent work—see pp. 140 and 388 of the Tenth Edition and the *Kingston-upon-Hull* case. The contractor had clearly breached the contract in at least two respects and the duty of supervision was owed to the employer and not to him, so that he could have no possible defence to the owner's action in dismissing him. This is not to say, of course, that the engineer may not also have been negligent.]

The practical position in these cases will now be radically changed in England by the new Civil Liability (Contribution) Act 1978, which will now enable defendants liable in contract to obtain contribution from other defendants in contract or tort (see *post* in this Supplement under pp. 306–310).

156–159 **Surveys.** The discussion at these pages is limited to building and valuation surveys. Site surveys and reports, which are a normal precursor to design and contract documents being prepared for both civil engineering and larger building projects are, of course, in a different category, and a number of cases arising out of them are referred to in the discussion in this Supplement under pp. 63–75. See also under pp. 90 and 133.

165–169 **The discussion at these pages** has now happily become largely academic. In *Sutcliffe* v. *Thakrah* [1974] A.C. 727, the defendants were acting as both architects and quantity surveyors, issuing certificates for interim payment in the usual way. The employer dismissed the contractor, who became insolvent. The employer then sued the architects for negligence in certifying for defective work and work which had not been done at all, as a result of which over-payments had been made. *Held* by the House of Lords, over-ruling *Chambers* v. *Goldthorpe*, that in certifying the architect was not an arbitrator, and could be liable for negligence.

The *Sutcliffe* case clearly applies equally to final certificates, or indeed any other form of certification. The opinions in the case are not, however, entirely clear as to the extent to which they are based on the certifier's function as it was described in the contract, or as it was actually performed in the event in the case before them. It is just possible that the case leaves open the position should an actual dispute be formulated before a certifier for his decision— see *per* Lord Morris particularly—or whether a contractual provision expressly contemplating such a dispute would be in a different position from a simple certifying provision. Again in *Arenson* v. *Casson, Beckman* [1977] A.C. 405 an uncle sold shares in his private company to his nephew, with a term that on leaving the company the shares should be re-transferred to the uncle at a price to be fixed by the company's auditors, whose decision should be final and binding. The provision made no mention of disputes. A re-sale took place under the contract, at a price one-sixth of the price at which the company's shares were sold when the company went public six months later. The nephew sued the auditors in tort. It was held by the House of Lords, distinguishing other valuer cases where the valuer was required by the contract wording to settle disputes, that the auditors had no immunity. This last case is of considerable importance, since it reinforces the possibility that *contractors* may now be free to sue certifiers in tort for carelessness in the issue of their certificates, at least where no dispute has been formulated, on the *Hedley Byrne* v. *Heller* principle. See also the discussion *supra* under pp. 63–75 in this Supplement.

SECTION 7. DUTIES AND LIABILITIES OF QUANTITY SURVEYORS

169 **Bills of Quantities.** See the author's full review of Bills under the United Kingdom forms and practices in the *Journal of Maritime Law and Commerce*, Washington D.C., Vol. 6, No. 3, April 1975, and the discussion in this Supplement *post* under p. 556.

Preliminary Items. A principal reason for the difficulties is that the Standard Methods of Measurement in the United Kingdom have been extremely lax in specifying precisely what items of expenditure should be so billed—see this Supplement *infra*, under p. 556.

171 **Function (iv).** For an excellent illustration of a case where the important distinction between variations and simple remeasurement was both vitally important and correctly appreciated by the courts, see the decision of the New South Wales Court of Appeal in *Arcos Industries* v. *Electricity Commission of N.S.W.* [1973] 2 N.S.W.L.R. 186, illustrated on this point *infra* in this Supplement under p. 514.

SECTION 9. REMUNERATION

190 Copyright. See *Chabot* v. *Davies* [1936] 3 All E.R. 221 (plan and elevation of shop-front held subject to copyright under the Act of 1911, and damages to be a reasonable licence fee for use of the copyright). Notwithstanding the architect's clear right to *ownership* of copyright, in the absence of express agreement to the contrary, the practical question will usually be the extent of the building owner's *licence* to use the copyright for his building.

ILLUSTRATIONS

(1) A building owner wished to use an architect's plans so as to complete the building in substantial accordance with them. *Held* by the New South Wales S.C. (Jacobs J.) that in the absence of express provision there was an implied licence to use the plans for this purpose, and, if not complete, to prepare such further drawings as might be required. The implied consent was also transferable to a purchaser on sale of the land: *Beck* v. *Montana Constructions Ltd.* [1964–65] N.S.W.L.R. 229.

(2) An architect prepared plans in order to obtain planning consent for a proposed building. His employment was then terminated on reasonable notice under the R.I.B.A. Conditions of Engagement. His plans were then used by the employer's surveyors to prepare detailed plans for by-law approval. Held by the Court of Appeal, applying *Beck* v. *Montana Constructions Ltd.*, that on payment of his fees on termination in accordance with the R.I.B.A. scale there was an implied licence to use the plans for these purposes: *Blair* v. *Osborne & Tomkins* [1971] 1 All E.R. 468.

(3) Planning permission had been refused for a factory, and an architect specialising in such difficult cases was engaged to prepare new plans, which contained an unusual and attractive feature, as a result of which permission was obtained. Later the owner employed another architect to build who adopted the plaintiff's special feature. The architect had charged a nominal fee of £100 (the R.I.B.A. scale at one-sixth would have been £900), marking it " nominal " in his account and expressly stating that copyright was retained and no use should be made of his plans without his consent. Held by the Court of Appeal, both the *Beck* and *Blair* cases involved full R.I.B.A. instalment fees being charged. On the facts no licence would be implied for the use of the plans in the later building, though clearly there was a licence for planning purposes. *Per* Salmon and Megaw L.JJ., an architect may agree considerably less than his full fee for a planning permission in a doubtful, case, since he knows there is a chance that the project and expense may be abortive. It would be unreasonable, if the project went ahead successfully, to imply a licence for use in construction without further charge: *Stovin-Bradford* v. *Volpoint* [1971] Ch. 1007.

CHAPTER 3 – TENDERS AND ESTIMATES

SECTION 1. TYPES OF TENDER DOCUMENTS

200– **Types of contract.** It may perhaps be emphasised that the actual
201 expressions used by the parties to describe their contract or its
documents may be misleading, and it will be the combined effect,
on their true construction, of all the contractual provisions and
documents which will determine the category to which it belongs.

For an interesting modern variant of category (2), where despite
the use of a fully priced schedule of quantities showing a grossed-up
total, the contract was in the lump sum or fixed price category,
with the exception of one item of work only, which was to be
remeasurable, see *Commissioner for Main Roads* v. *Reed and
Stuart* (1974) 48 A.L.J.R. 461 illustrated in this Supplement under
p. 514.

For an example of category (4), where the contract stated " This
is a Schedule of Rates Contract " but in fact a fully grossed-up
" Schedule of Quantities and Rates " producing an exactly calculated contract price, was used, so that it was a remeasurement
contract indistinguishable for all legal and practical purposes from
category (3), see *Arcos Industries* v. *Electricity Commission of
N.S.W.* [1973] 2 N.S.W.L.R. 186, illustrated in this Supplement
under p. 514.

One (purely practical) difference where quantities are not known
in contracts in category (4) is that the extent of remeasurement
will be greater, since in other cases remeasurement is usually
directed in practice at calculating differences from the contract
quantities rather than full remeasurement *de novo*. A legal difference may be that there will be little or no need for a variation
clause, or only for strictly limited purposes.

203 **Preliminary Items.** See the discussion *post* in this Supplement
under p. 556.

204 **A third reason for billing work under a " provisional sum "** may
be that, for one reason or another, it has not been possible to
design or otherwise define the work precisely at the time of
contracting.

205 **Suggested usage for P.C. or Provisional Sums.** This receives considerable support from the following interesting case.

ILLUSTRATION

A main contract was in a lump sum form, and itself expressly excluded any fluctuations clause. Part of the specification stated " Claims by sub-contractors will not be considered relative to rise and fall. The Builder will pay all such claims and allow for this in his tender." Clause 21 of the printed conditions provided in the usual way for the substitution in the accounts of any additional amounts " properly expended in respect of prime cost or provisional sums." The architect nominated a sub-contractor whose quotation included a fluctuations clause. *Held*, by the High Court of Australia, that the specification was probably an old document, and that the builder was entitled to recover the fluctuations payable to the nominated sub-contractor. *Per* Stephen J.: " I would require a most clearly expressed provision to overcome the inference that when a proprietor requires a builder to accept his estimate of the cost of an item by including P.C. sums as a mandatory part of the tender, those P.C. amounts, which are only estimates made for the purpose of convenience, are inherently subject to adjustment when the true cost . . . emerges in due course ": *Tuta Products* v. *Hutcherson Bros.* (1972) 46 A.L.J.R. 119.

The new (Fifth) English I.C.E. conditions now contain (cl. 58) satisfactory and clear definitions of the two expressions, and a clear statement of the engineer's powers in relation to them. This is the first United Kingdom standard form to achieve either of these objects.

212 Cost-plus contracts. See the interesting treatment of English Government practice as to these, in particular in regard to the percentages adopted in *Government Contracts*, by Colin Turpin, at pp. 176–178 and 188–192. There are many cases on these contracts in United States jurisdictions, dealing particularly with which heads of expense should be included in " cost " and which in the percentage: see Am.Jur. (2d), Vol. 13, para. 20.

SECTION 2.   INCORPORATION OF DOCUMENTS

214 Add illustration (5).

ILLUSTRATION

(5) An order from a main contractor to nominated sub-contractors required them " To supply . . . labour plant and machinery . . . in full accordance with the appropriate form for Nominated Sub-Contractors R.I.B.A. 1965 Edition." (The description of the form was wrong and evidence was received to identify it—see this Supplement, *ante* under p. 56). *Held*, the words were sufficient to incorporate the arbitration clause in the

(correctly identified) form of sub-contract: *Modern Buildings* v. *Limmer & Trinidad* [1975] 1 W.L.R. 1281. (For a case of *implied* incorporation of plant-hirer's " usual conditions " into a contract, see also the *British Crane Hire* case in this Supplement, *ante* under p. 56.)

Footnote 34a. Reference should be to A.L.J.R.

Third paragraph and Footnote 38a. The *Gleeson* appeal was not proceeded with. See however the case of *English Industrial Estates* v. *George Wimpey* (1972) 71 L.G.R. 127; 7 B.L.R. 126, and the discussion in this Supplement, *ante* under pp. 57–58.

215 **Footnote 43.** Reference should also be made to *Boot* v. *L.C.C.* [1959] 1 W.L.R. 1069, Chapter 1, p. 34, and for the effect of payment on interim certificate to Chapter 7, p. 493.

SECTION 3. ACCEPTANCE OF TENDER

217 **Subject to contract or to formal contract.** See the further cases referred to in this Supplement, *ante* under p. 16. See also *Chitty on Contracts* (23rd Edition), pp. 78–82.

220 **Conditions as to approval** can, of course, be waived, like many other contractual provisions, particularly where the work has been carried out.

ILLUSTRATION

A sub-contract provided " This Agreement subject to approval of the Toowoomba City Council." Approval had been given on the expressed condition that the Council should not be deemed to have notice of or approve differences in the unit-prices between the main and sub-contract. *Held* by the High Court of Australia, when granting rectification of the sub-contract (as to which see the case illustrated in this Supplement, *ante* under p. 38) and dealing with the difficulty that the rectified contract had not been approved, that since the sub-contract had been fully executed the parties could be treated as having waived the condition. Alternatively, if there was no contract because the failure to approve operated as a suspensory condition, the plaintiff could recover on an implied contract or *quantum meruit*, with the contract as evidence of what was reasonable remuneration: *M. R. Hornibrook (Pty) Ltd.* v. *Eric Newham* (1971) 45 A.L.J.R. 523. (See also *City of Box Hill* v. *E. W. Tauschke* (1974) V.R. 39 illustrated, *infra* under p. 225).

225 **Add second illustration:**

(2) A contractor's tender for roadworks provided: " The Council will by notice under the hand of the Town Clerk certify

its acceptance of the tender and the successful tenderer shall
within 4 days . . . execute the contract and/or sign the General
Conditions containing all special stipulations terms and conditions
as the Council may deem necessary to impose for the purpose of
carrying out the said contract. . . ." The tender was accepted
unconditionally on March 16, 1965, but the contractor did not
sign the formal contract and conditions until July 21, 1965, by
which time the Contractor had completed £7,000 worth of work
out of £36,000, and received progress payments, and an accident
had occurred in which a passer-by was injured due to a dangerous
condition caused by the work. The employer wished to rely on an
indemnity clause in the Conditions, but it was objected that at the
time of the accident no contract had been signed. *Held* by Pope J.
(S.C. of Victoria) (a) since the Council had made no attempt to
impose further conditions there was a binding contract when the
tender was accepted, but if this was wrong, and the contract was
not concluded until July, there was, following *Trollope & Colls* v.
Atomic Power, an implied term that it should have retrospective
effect: *City of Box Hill* v. *E. W. Tauschke* [1974] V.R. 39.

228 **Part (4).** Add text before illustrations as follows: It has been
said that contracts of this type might on acceptance form a contract to buy the stipulated quantities; on the other hand they might
impose an obligation to sell but not to buy; and that an intermediate
type might impose an obligation to buy all the purchaser's requirements but subject to that without obligation as to quantity: see
per Atkin J. in *Percival* v. *L.C.C. Asylums* (1918) 87 L.J.Q.B. 677.

Footnote 83. Add: Followed by Atkin J. in *Percival's* case *supra.*

229 **Add at end of Section 3:** See also the case of *Cana Construction* v.
The Queen (1973) 37 D.L.R. (3d) 418, illustrated in this Supplement, *post* under p. 551, where an estimated quantity of work
was held to be a warranty of amount within 10 per cent in either
direction.

SECTION 4. LIABILITY APART FROM CONTRACT

230 **Illustrations.** See also *Turriff Construction* v. *Regalia Knitting
Mills* (H.H. Judge Edgar Fay) (1971) 222 E.G. 169; [1972] C.L.Y.
461.

234 **Collusive tendering and Act of 1968.** The Court can declare
unregistered agreements void if against public policy, and the
employer has a right to damages if the agreement is not disclosed
to the registrar—see section 7 of the Act.

CHAPTER 5 – PERFORMANCE

SECTION 1. OBLIGATIONS OF THE CONTRACTOR

250 **Second paragraph.** Availability of remedy of substantial performance if work abandoned. The remedy would not be available under
South African law where abandonment before completion, or a
method of performance inconsistent with an honest intention to
carry out the contract, occurs: *Hauman* v. *Nortje* [1914] A.D. 293,
at p. 297 and *Breslin* v. *Hichens* [1914] A.D. 312.

254 **Add illustration (11).**

A plumbing and heating contractor contracted to design and
instal a heating system for £560. The system had defects which
would cost £174 to repair. As installed, the system gave out fumes
when switched on, making the living rooms uncomfortable, and
due to insufficient radiators and insulation the heating was
inadequate by 10 per cent and in some rooms by 25 per cent–30
per cent. The contractor refused to remedy the defects when
complaint was made. The County Court judge found substantial
performance as a fact. *Held* by the Court of Appeal, the plaintiff
contractor could not recover. *Per* Cairns L.J., both the nature and
amount of the defects were far different from those in *Dakin* v.
Lee. Per Sachs L.J., the general ineffectiveness of the work for
its purpose, rather than the number of defects, led to the conclusion. The plaintiff had only himself to blame, since he could
have remedied the defects of which he received complaints so as
to earn his money. *Held*, also, that the defendant was entitled to
£15 damages for inconvenience: *Bolton* v. *Mahadeva* [1972] 1
W.L.R. 1009.

268– **Contractor's unqualified obligation to complete.** The law in a
269 number of jurisdictions in the United States appears to be less
severe than that exemplified by the *Thorn* and *Tharsis* cases, for
example, where difficulties during construction can be shown to be
caused exclusively by the architects' or engineers' design and not in
any way contributed to by the contractor: see *e.g. Bentley* v. *The
State* (1889) 41 N.W. 338 (Sp.Ct. of Wisconsin); *Penn Bridge* v.
City of New Orleans (1915) 222 F. 733 (U.S. 5th Circuit C.A.); and
U.S. v. *Spearin* (1918) 248 U.S. 132 (Sp.Ct. of U.S.)—though in
some jurisdictions the English view has prevailed—*Lonergan* v.
San Antonio Loan & Trust (1907) 104 S.W. 1061 (Sp.Ct. of Texas).

Moreover, cases of unexpected site difficulties calling for later
design changes have frequently been treated in the same way, even
where additional expense or delay, rather than total impracticability
or a change of design, result: see *Christie* v. *U.S.* (1915) 237 U.S.

234 (Sp.Ct. U.S.) and *Montrose Contracting Co.* v. *City of West-chester* (1936) 80 F. (2d) 841 (U.S. C of A., 2d Circuit). Some of the United States decisions even appear to over-ride express contractual provisions or disclaimers: see *e.g. Hollenbach* v. *U.S.* (1914) 233 U.S. 165 (Sp.Ct. of U.S.); *U.S.* v. *Atlantic Dredging* (1920) 253 U.S.1 (appeal from U.S. Ct. of Claims); *Maney* v. *City of Oklahoma* (1931) 300 P. 642 (Sp.Ct. of Oklahoma); *Young & Fehlhaber Pile Co.* v. *State of New York* (1941) 177 Misc. 204, and the *Montrose* case *supra.*

The factual background of some civil engineering contracts, where the opportunity for investigation by tendering contractors may be extremely limited and the only real investigations will have been carried out by the employer's advisers, and where the engineer's permanent design may be at least partly dictated by considerations of the temporary working methods thought to be most desirable, may perhaps justify the implication of an appropriate term warrantying the practicability of the design in a particular instance where a contractor is, to the knowledge of the employer, as a fact compelled to rely on the architect or engineer, and has no means of ascertaining or investigating the risks involved. Contracts are in any case likely to have express provisions either insisting on full contractor's responsibility on the one hand, or permitting claims for varied work or for additional or unforeseen expense on the other. This seems to be an area where some reconsideration by the English Courts in cases involving special facts and no express provision, may be overdue.

270 **Jackson's case.** Contrast *U.S.* v. *Spearin, supra* under pp. 268–9.

271 **Nuttall and Lynton case.** Contrast *Maney* v. *City of Oklahoma, supra* under pp. 268–9.

274– **For the precise " minimum " standard** represented by the " mer-
275 chantability " warranties see *Hardwick Game Farms* v. *S.A.P.P.A.* [1969] 2 A.C. 31.

275 **Liability absolute and independent of fault.** See also the United States cases discussed *infra* in this Supplement under p. 290.

282 **Last sentence of second paragraph.** See however the difficult decision of the Supreme Court of Canada in *Brunswick Construction*

v. *Nowlan* (1975 49 D.L.R. (3d) 93, illustrated in this Supplement, *infra* under p. 288.

287 **Add further illustration** after *Lynch* v. *Thorne* and re-number following illustrations:

(12) An employer changed a roof specification so as to permit the alternative use of a laminated wood structure. Specialist suppliers then immediately approached the main contractor with a proposed design conforming to the altered specification. The employer's officers then discussed and determined the final design together with the supplier, and the contractor then placed an order. The structure proved unsuitable and the contractor sued the supplier for damages. It was objected that there had been no reliance on the supplier by the contractor. *Held* by S.C. of Canada, following *Myers* v. *Brent Cross Garage*, it was not necessary to show exclusive reliance, and it was sufficient that the reliance had acted as a substantial and effective inducement to purchase from the supplier: *Laminated Structures* v. *Eastern Woodworkers Ltd.* (1962) 32 D.L.R. (2d) 1.

288 **Add further illustrations.**

(15) Specialists in burglar-proof protection contracted to supply a steel door to suit an existing soft-wood door frame in a brick wall, together with locking bars engaging into the brickwork. Thieves broke in by prising out the soft-wood jambs. *Held* by the High Court of Australia (the minority dissenting only on the facts) overruling the Court of Appeal of N.S.W. (who had held that the door as supplied complied exactly with its description in the quotation " to suit opening " and that no term could be implied to supply protection over the wider area of the existing wooden door frame) and applying *Myers* v. *Brent Cross Garage*, that there was an implied term to supply and fit a door which, by whatever means, would provide reasonable protection against persons seeking to break in: *Reg Glass* v. *Rivers Locking Systems* (1968) 120 C.L.R. 516.

(16) A specialist contractor undertook to build the structural steel frame and roof-deck of a shopping mall in accordance with the architect's drawings and to supply design drawings of his own work for approval by the architect. The contractor submitted his drawings, with the roof loadings expressly indicated, after discussions with the owner's project manager, who had agreed them subject to the approval of the architect and their compliance with the Building Code. They were approved by the architect, but the described loadings did not at certain points comply with the Code and the building was overstressed and deflected excessively in certain snow conditions, though not actually unsafe. *Held* by the Appellate Division of the New Brunswick S.C., that the architect was engaged to design the architectural envelope of the building, and his duty was to see that the contractor-designed part of the structure complied with his own specified dimensions. Nothing in these facts relieved the contractor from his responsibility for

properly designing the steel structure: *Acme Investments Ltd.* v. *York Structural Steel Ltd.* (1974) 9 N.B.R. (2d) 699.

[*Note*: This case illustrates, entirely correctly, it is submitted, the often limited scope of approvals where the matter concerned lies outside the expertise of the person giving approval. Had the drawings been required to be submitted to a structural engineer of the employer, other considerations might, depending on the wording, have applied.]

(17) A building owner without any professional adviser supplied builders with plans for a building, asking only that the roof should be tiled and not iron as shown on the plans. The builder carried out the amended work in exact accordance with the plans but without altering the inner construction of the roof, which as a consequence was too weak to carry the weight of the tiles. *Held* by the S.C. of South Africa (Van Rhyn J.), that there appeared to be no difference on this point between the law of England and South Africa and, not following *Lynch* v. *Thorne*, that there was an implied term that the tiled roof should be properly constructed: *Colin* v. *De Guisti* [1975] 4 S.A.L.R. 223.

(18) A building owner commissioned an architect to prepare a plan for a dwelling house. The contract provided that "the Engineer" should have general supervision and direction, but that the contractor should have complete control of his own organisation subject to Article 11. That Article provided "The Contractor shall give efficient supervision to the work using his best skill and attention." At some stage not disclosed in the report it was decided to dispense with the architect for supervision purposes, and the owner was content to rely on the builder. There was no proper specification, and the plans made no provision for ventilation of the roof space or for the erection of air spaces. Extensive rotting developed due to condensation. The building was then reconstructed with a different type of window. *Held* by the Supreme Court of Canada (Dickson J. dissenting) that the contractor must be taken to have accepted the fact that the owner was relying on his skill and judgment, particularly having regard to the provisions of Article 11. A contractor with his experience should have recognised the defects in the plans, and was under a duty to warn the owner of the danger inherent in executing the architect's plans: *Brunswick Construction* v. *Nowlan* (1975) 49 D.L.R. (3d) 93.

[*Note*: This is a difficult case, and looks wrong in principle. Much might turn on the precise stage at which the contractor was informed that the architect would not be further employed on the project, and the exact degree of development of the architect's design at that stage, since the failure alleged is one at the design, not supervision, stage. Confidence in the majority judgment is considerably reduced (a) by the reference to Article 11, which is a common-form type of provision for adequate site superintendence found in normal contracts where architects are employed in the usual way, and therefore seems to have no relevance to a possible express assumption of abnormal duties of design by the contractor and (b) by reference in the majority judgments to the last paragraph of the Tenth Edition of Hudson at p. 291, *infra*, which is concerned with *express* assumptions of responsibilities by contractors. Dickson J. in his dissenting judgment referred, it is respectfully submitted rightly on the facts disclosed in the report, to the last sentence of the second paragraph of p. 282 of the Tenth Edition as being the appropriate proposition to apply when stating "There is nothing in the

> contract which imposes a duty on the contractor to detect faults in the
> design plans prepared by the owner's architects, or impose a duty to inform
> the owners that the plans are faulty in design."]

290 **Liability absolute and independent of fault** (reputable sub-contractors and sources of supply). The law in the United States has also turned in the opposite direction. On this see *Wisconsin Red Pressed Brick* v. *Hood* (1897) 69 N.W. 1091, followed in *Flannery* v. *St. Louis Architectural Iron* (1916) 185 S.W. 760; *Whaley* v. *Milton* (1951) 241 S.W. (2d) 23, and *Wood-Hopkins* v. *Masonry Contractors* (1970) 235 So. (2d) 548; but see now *contra Aced* v. *Hobbs-Sesack* (1961) 7 Cal.Rep. 391, and *Smith* v. *Old Warson Development Co.* (1972) 479 S.W. (2d) 795 (Supreme Court of Missouri—" we believe fault or negligence by warrantor no longer required for recovery under implied warranty ").

293 **Footnote 82.** Add additional reference (1966) 58 D.L.R. (2d) 595. **Add at end of second paragraph.** For an additional (and doubtful) case which a majority of the Supreme Court of Canada treated as based on express undertakings by the contractor, see the case of *Brunswick Construction* v. *Nowlan* (illustrated, *supra* in this Supplement under p. 288).

300 **Reword first paragraph** of text so as to refer to the penultimate case, and add further illustration (6) as follows:

> (6) H, owners of a helicopter which crashed due to a defective retaining bolt of the tail rotor-blade, sued R, their wholly-owned subsidiary, with whom they had an oral agreement for the servicing of the machine. It was an oral or implied term of the contract that the defendants would when necessary obtain certified spare parts from the manufacturer's distributor. It was not practicable to test for latent defects. The bolt in question came from the approved source with all the appropriate certification, but contained a latent defect which was the cause of the crash. *Held* by the High Court of Australia, that H, knowing of R's limited technical capabilities, and of the provenance of the replacement parts, made a stipulation as to quality which it regarded as of greater weight than anything of which R was capable. It was this for which H bargained and no necessity arose for the operation of an implied warranty of quality. *Per* Barwick C.J.: H knew that a new certified bolt made by the Bell Helicopter Co. to a particular specification and imported into Australia would be used by R . . . no further warranty was intended. *Per* Stephen J.: In the *Young and Marten* case, it was recognised that the exclusion of a warranty of quality was more readily possible where the supply of goods was only incidental to the services performed. The present contract was predominantly for the performance of

engineering services in maintenance and overhauling of H's aircraft, the servicing of parts being an incidental albeit important feature of R's contractual obligations: *Helicopter Sales (Australia) Pty. Ltd.* v. *Rotor-Work Pty. Ltd.* (1974) 48 A.L.J.R. 390.

[*Note:* This case seems, with the greatest respect, inconsistent with policy, principle and authority. Much of the language of the judgments seems relevant only to an implied warranty of *suitability*—not to the minimum standard of *merchantability*, where reliance is surely usually irrelevant. The decision ignores the vital " chain of responsibility " principle enunciated in the *Young and Marten* case, from which, as from *Myers* v. *Brent Cross*, the case seems virtually indistinguishable. The Court seems to have attached great weight to the expectation or requirement, in an informal agreement, that manufacturer's parts, with certified testing cerificates, would be invariably used. If the certificates were to be issued *to the plaintiffs* that might perhaps be a factor removing the need for any implied term. But it is hard to see how certificates issued to the defendants, which would be valueless to the plaintiffs in the event of faults being found, could negative the implied term.]

(7) The Specification for the supply of a television mast, together with all the associated electronic services including aerial and feeder systems, provided by clause 2.1: " The aerial support structure shall be designed and supplied by B . . ." E, the main contractor, obtained a quotation from B, who were experts in the field of very tall hollow stressed-skin metal masts, before themselves quoting to the employer I, and did so (in relation to the mast) in terms of quoting a price " for the design supply and delivery " of the mast. E were specialist manufacturers of electronic equipment and could have no experience of masts of the specified type, which were themselves in a new technology field. The mast collapsed, due to the inadequacy of its design, when the stays were exposed to combined icing and winds. I sued E, who contended that there was no obligation on him at all in regard to the design of the mast, or, alternatively, that if there was, he should be under no greater duty than a professional man, namely a duty of reasonable care and skill. *Held* by the Court of Appeal (Roskill L.J.) that, applying the chain of liability principle in the *Pryor* and *Hardwick Game Farm* cases, there was an implied term in the main contract that the mast should be reasonably fit for its purpose, namely that, irrespective of negligence, it should be proof against any meteorological conditions likely to be encountered, and since the particular weather conditions were likely to occur once every three or four years, E was liable to I in contract. *Per* Roskill L.J. " in the case of successive construction contracts the ultimate liability if something goes wrong should rest where it properly belongs . . . ." *I.B.A.* v. *E.M.I. Ltd. and B.I.C.C. Ltd.* (1978) C.A. (unreported).

[*Note:* It is understood at the time of going to print that this case is under appeal to the House of Lords, but in view of its very great potential importance it has been included in this Supplement. It is respectfully submitted that the decision is right and accords with both authority and principle.]

306 Indemnity provisions. These may take the form of indemnifying the other party against the breach of some obligation or group of obligations, in which event, as a matter of semantics, it could be argued that the provision, though expressed as an indemnity, represents little more than the stipulation or repetition of the contractual obligation itself. On the other hand the indemnity may be expressed in relation to a defined class of claim, loss, damage, or expense (often, of course, itself the result of a breach of contract). The distinction may be important, since it has been argued that, for purposes of limitation, the cause of action (the starting point of the period under English law) arises on the breach or other event in the former case, while it is quite clear that in the latter case it will not arise until the time of damage or loss, or the receipt and payment of a claim, or when the liability is " ascertained or established "—see *Collinge* v. *Heywood* (1839) 9 Ad. & Ell. 633. McNair J. considered that in the former case the earlier date of the relevant contractual breach might apply—see *Bosma* v. *Larsen* [1966] 1 Lloyd's Rep. 22—but in *County and District Properties* v. *Jenner* [1976] 2 Lloyd's Rep. 728 Swanwick J., after an exhaustive examination of the authorities, disagreed with this, and, while dissecting the group of indemnities given by sub-contractors to main contractors in clause 3 of the F.A.S.S. standard form of sub-contract into the two different classes, held that the later date applied to both classes in a case where an employer sued a main contractor for defective work and the latter invoked the indemnity clauses in their sub-contracts when joining a number of sub-contractors in third party proceedings.

306–
310 The discussion on these pages will at a number of points require re-consideration following the coming into force in England of the Civil Liability (Contribution) Act 1978, which replaces section 6 of the Law Reform Act of 1935, and now confers a right to contribution by a person liable in respect of any damage against any person liable for the same damage, whatever the basis of liability in contract tort or otherwise of either party (see s. 6 (1) of the 1978 Act) from January 1, 1979.

The Act is not, however, to affect any express or implied contractual right to indemnity or any express contractual provision regulating or excluding contribution (see s. 7 (3)). The Act would seem clearly to apply to contribution in respect of a liability established in an arbitration, or to settlements made in respect of a claim in an arbitration (in the latter case, as in settlements of High Court proceedings, provided the factual basis of the claim, if established, would create liability against the person seeking the contribution (see s. 1 (4)).) One possible difference in regard to arbitrations may be that awards in an arbitration in favour of the person against whom contribution is sought may not be binding on the person seeking contribution in the same way as a judgment in a court (see s. 1 (5)).

The practical importance of the Act, in the light of the well-known difficulties created by the separate liabilities, often in contract, of the various parties involved in a building or engineering project, cannot be over-emphasised. The existence of this new right is bound, for example, to constrain the Courts, when assessing claims to contribution between architects and contractors in respect of claims by the employer, indirectly to evolve a new area of responsibility or duty as between the two (where previously none, of course, existed) when giving effect to the " just and equitable " test for contribution laid down by the Act (see s. 2 (1)). (As in the case of the 1935 Act, the contribution may, in appropriate cases, amount to a complete indemnity). The application of this test, for example, to an architect's claim for contribution against a contractor in respect of defective work where the basis of the claim against the architect was failure to supervise, or to the claim, so often advanced unsuccessfully by contractors in the past, that the architect might have detected or condemned work at an earlier stage, or could have mitigated damage by ordering a variation to assist the contractor in a difficulty, may be expected to be a source of great interest.

308 **Walters v. Whessoe.** See [1968] 1 W.L.R. 1056, and now also reported in 6 B.L.R. 23. The case has now been followed and approved by the House of Lords in *Smith* v. *South Wales Switchgear* [1978] 1 W.L.R. 165, and the principle can no longer be regarded as in doubt in England in spite of the hesitation expressed in the Tenth Edition.

309 **Amend first line** of text so as to delete reference to " last decision " and substitute reference to *A.M.F.* case.

Add further illustrations:

(5) Scaffolding sub-contractors indemnified a main contractor against " any liability . . . whatsoever . . . in respect of personal injuries . . . arising out of or happening in connection with the execution of the work . . . by reason of any default or omission

on our part." A workman was injured due to a mains cable left hanging carelessly in the way by the main contractor's workmen, and the plaintiff sued both main and sub-contractors as co-defendants. No complaint had been made by the sub-contractor to the main contractor, who was in control of the site. *Held* by McKenna J., both defendants were negligent, and " default etc." in the clause related to the injuries, not the liability. Even if it related to liability, the sub-contractor's failure to complain was a sufficient connection with the main contractor's liability, since but for it the accident could have been avoided, and it was not necessary for it to be an essential element in the workman's claim against the main contractor, who was therefore entitled to an indemnity from the sub-contractor. *Per* McKenna J.: " I have not found these questions of construction easy and I have no great confidence in my answers to them ": *Smith* v. *Vange Scaffolding* [1970] 1 W.L.R. 733.

(6) A customer indemnified a carrier against " all claims or demands whatsoever " in excess of the carrier's liability to the customer under the conditions. *Held* by the Court of Appeal, this included claims due to the carrier's negligence: *Gillespie Bros.* v. *Roy Bowles Transport Ltd.* [1973] 1 Q.B. 400.

(7) By clause 18 (2) of the then current R.I.B.A. conditions the main contractor indemnified the employer for damage to property provided that it was caused by the " negligence omission or default of the contractor his servants or agents or of any sub-contractor." The employer received claims by meat-trader occu-piers of the building, which was an abattoir, for spoiled meat. The damage had been caused by a proprietary product which nominated sub-contractors had been ordered by the architect to purchase from a specialist supplier for the purpose of water-proofing the floors. *Held* by Kerr J. (a) that on the facts the damage had been caused by both the negligence and the default of the sub-sub-supplier of the product, who had advised the use of one of his range of products with wrong advice as to curing times, but (b) the indemnity clause must be construed strictly in the same way as an exception clause (following *Gillespie Brothers* v. *Roy Bowles Transport Ltd.* [1973] 1 Q.B. 400 and *Canada S.S. Ltd.* v. *The King* [1952] A.C. 192), and since there was no negligence or default by the main contractor or the nominated sub-contractor (or, *semble* even by a servant or agent of the sub-contractor, had these words been present) the employer could not rely on the clause. *Per* Kerr J., " default " in this context is involved if a person either does not do what he ought to do or does what he ought not to do, provided that something in the nature of a breach of duty is involved so as to be properly describable as a default: *City of Manchester* v. *Fram Gerrard* (1974) 6 B.L.R. 71.

(8) Hirers of a crane which was to be driven by the owner's driver undertook by Condition 6 to be responsible for recovery of the crane from soft ground, and by Condition 8 to indemnify the owner " against all expenses in connection with or arising out of the use of the plant." The crane became bogged down due to the driver ignoring instructions of the hirer's site agent. *Held* by

the Court of Appeal, neither clause was wide enough to include the negligence of the owner's driver: *British Crane Hire* v. *Ipswich Plant Hire* [1975] Q.B. 303 (See also *Farr* v. *Admiralty* at p. 312 of the Tenth Edition).

310 **Insert after second paragraph** the following new paragraph and illustrations:

Indemnity clauses are often expressed in very general terms. Wherever possible they will be construed restrictively so as to be limited to cases where the party giving the indemnity is at fault.

ILLUSTRATIONS

(1) A seller of teapots undertook " to protect the purchaser against all claims losses damages costs and expenses which arise from or occur as a result of the sales against any item purchased." The buyer compromised a claim by a badly burnt girl in view of the possibility of astronomical claims if the jury found for the plaintiff. *Held* by the Ontario Court of Appeal, despite the general words the seller had not undertaken that no one would sue the buyer, but only to meet established liabilities to subsequent purchasers. The words should be restricted to claims arising from the implied conditions of merchantability and fitness, and since as a fact there were no defects in the teapot, the buyer could not recover: *Helfand* v. *Royal Canadian Art Pottery* (1970) 11 D.L.R. (3d) 404.

(2) A main contractor for roadworks indemnified the employer against " all claims for injury . . . which may arise out of or in consequence of the works and against all claims . . . damages costs whatsoever in respect thereof or in relation thereto," and a sub-contractor indemnified the main contractor against " any loss liability claim or proceedings . . . arising out of or in the course of or caused by the execution of the works." An injured passer-by failed in his legally-aided claim against the employer and main contractor, on the ground that he had caused his own injury and had not, as he alleged, fallen into unguarded excavations. *Held* by the Court of Appeal, neither the employer nor the main contractor could recover their legal costs under their respective indemnity clauses: *Richardson* v. *Buckinghamshire C.C.* [1971] 1 Lloyd's Rep. 533; (1971) 69 L.G.R. 327.

311 **Add illustrations:**

(3) Clause 15B of the Australian Standard Form provided that " the existing structures " and the works should be at the sole risk of the employer as regards loss and damage by fire. By clause 14 (C) the contractor indemnified the employer for injury and damage to property provided it was due to the contractor's negligence and " subject as regards loss or damage by fire, to clause 15B." The contractor was to work on existing premises part of which was owned by the employer, and the remainder of which was leased by the employer from the owner of adjoining land.

A fire caused by the contractor's negligence damaged both parts of the property. *Held* by the High Court of Australia, the employer could not recover for his own loss as lessee of the adjoining property and must pay the contractor to rebuild it, since it was all part of "the existing structures," but the contractor had no claim against the employer in respect of his own liability to the adjoining freeholder, since the object of clause 15B was to safeguard the contractor from claims by the employer for damage to the employer's property in the works, not against claims by third parties: *K. D. Morris & Sons* v. *G. J. Coles* (1972) 46 A.L.J.R. 464.

312 **Farr's case.** Compare illustrations (5) (6) and (7) *supra* in this Supplement under p. 309.

314 **Notice of Claims.** Footnote 45. In addition to *Terson's* case, refer to *A. MacAlpine & Son* v. *Transvaal Provincial Administration* [1974] 3 S.A.L.R. 506, illustrated on this point *infra* in this Supplement under p. 536.

SECTION 2. OBLIGATIONS OF THE EMPLOYER

316– **State of the site.** See now, however, the greatly expanded duties
317 in tort for negligence causing purely economic loss, commented on at length in this Supplement under pp. 63–75, and the references to United States law in this particular context in this Supplement under pp. 268–269. See in particular the cases referred to under pp. 63–75 seeking to establish liability in tort in favour of the contractor, including *Miller* v. *Dames & Moore* (1961) 198 C.A. (2d) 305, and *Morrison-Knudsen International* v. *The Commonwealth* (1972) 46 A.L.J.R. 265.

317 **Footnote 54.** Reference for the *Twickenham* case is now [1971] Ch. 233. The *Twickenham* appeal was not proceeded with. The case has been criticised in 87 L.Q.R. 309–312, powerfully disapproved and not followed by Mahon J. in New Zealand, and not followed by Helsham J. in New South Wales. It is respectfully submitted that the *Twickenham* case can only be regarded as wrongly decided—see the cases and discussion in this Supplement *infra* under p. 712, including a directly contrary decision in Victoria at about the same time as the *Twickenham* case.

318 " **The site** " need not, of course, be co-terminous with the possibly greater area of the land owned or controlled by the employer, and may not always be visually recognisable as an entity. Greater precision than the simple use of the expression is needed in many contracts. Furthermore in many larger contracts, whether building or civil engineering, successive possession of parts of the site may be all that the contractor requires—see *e.g.* clause 42 of the English I.C.E. Conditions, which expressly contemplates this possibility. Each case, therefore, may require to be assessed carefully on its particular facts, whatever language may be used in the contract, and and the formulation of any too simplified implied terms for possession of " the whole site " should be avoided.

319 **Footnote 62a.** Add: in particular the *Pigott* and *Swanson* cases illustrated at pp. 338–339 of the Tenth Edition.

Carr's case. Reference should be to (1953 27 A.L.J.R. 273, and 89 C.L.R. 327. Tribunal was High Court of Australia.

323 **Time for instructions and information.** For the most careful general formulation to date, it is submitted, see the judgments of the Appellate Division in South Africa in *A. MacAlpine & Son* v. *Transvaal Provincial Administration* [1974] 3 S.A.L.R. 506, *supra* in this Supplement under p. 137. For a similar interpretation of an obligation to supply drawings " as work progresses " see *Fischbach and Moore of Canada* v. *Noranda Mines* (1978) 84 D.L.R. (3d) 465 (Sask. C.A.).

324 **First paragraph, last sentence.** Substitute " One solution may be " for " It is submitted that." Refer also to possible approach indicated at p. 763, where it is suggested that in these situations it may still be possible to hold the main contractor liable for the sub-contractor's breaches.

323– **Contractor's arguments.** These same arguments are frequently
325 advanced in regard to defective work. The problem is exacerbated by the fact that the United Kingdom standard forms without exception confer totally inadequate express powers on architects or engineers to deal with defective work, since they are almost invariably confined to ordering removal (or demolition) followed by reconstruction, whereas in practice, particularly with serious defects or defects discovered at a comparatively late stage, the practical requirement to avoid delay and undue expense for all parties may be to vary the design or specification.

CHAPTER 5 – PERFORMANCE

327 **Time for ordering instructions.** See the confirmation of the views here expressed in the Appellate Division of South Africa in *A. MacAlpine & Son* v. *Transvaal Provincial Administrator, supra* in this Supplement under p. 137. See also for a similar interpretation of an express term for information " as work progresses " *Fischbach and Moore of Canada* v. *Noranda Mines* (1978) 84 D.L.R. (3d) 465 (Sask, C.A.).

337 **The Bickerton decision** can have no application, of course, in the face of such express provisions as those in the GC/Wks/1 United Kingdom Government contract—see clauses 31 (2) and (3) and 38 (5) of that contract.

SECTION 3. DISCHARGE FROM FURTHER PERFORMANCE

341 **" Conditions."** The actual use of this expression in a contractual provision will not, however, necessarily mean that the provision in question falls into that special legal category: see *Wickman Machine Tool Sales* v. *Schuler* [1974] A.C. 235.

345 **Carr's case.** Reference should be to (1953) 27 A.L.J.R. 273 and (89) C.L.R. 327. Tribunal was High Court of Australia.

347 **Footnote 60.** Add: *Heyman's* case was followed in Victoria (Pope J.) in *Building and Engineering Constructions (Australia) Ltd.* v. *Property Securities* [1960] V.R. 673.

Add to first paragraph:

See, however, *Bloemen Ltd.* v. *Gold Coast City Pty. Ltd.* [1973] A.C. 115 (P.C.) where the Privy Council, on appeal from the High Court of Australia, held that a contractual provision for interest on all sums due under a contract would no longer apply in respect of a period after a repudiation had been accepted.

348 **See the recent " settled account " cases** and *Foakes* v. *Beer*, illustrated *ante* in this Supplement under pp. 19 and 23.

349 **Second paragraph.** See also the discussion on common mistake at pp. 26–27 of the Tenth Edition.

353 **Frustration.** Add illustration at end of second paragraph:

CHAPTER 5 – PERFORMANCE

ILLUSTRATION

A contractor sued for liquidated damages for delay, pleading that strikes had frustrated the provisions of the contract relating to delay and extension of time. *Held* by the S.C. of Victoria (Menhennitt J.), that, following *Hirji Mulji* v. *Cheong Yu* [1926] A.C. 497, frustration cannot apply to some but not all of a contract's provisions: *Aurel Forras* v. *Graham Karp Developments* [1975] V.R. 202.

Footnote 85. Add: See also for an example of a change in the law as a ground of frustration, *Industrial Overload* v. *McWatters* (1972) 24 D.L.R. (3d) 231 (Sask. Q.B., Sirois J.).

363 Illegality and irrecoverable instalments. The position is the same in United States jurisdictions: see *e.g. Comet Theatre Enterprises* v. *Cartwright* (9th Circuit C.A.) 195 F (2d) 80, 30 A.L.R. (2d) 1229.

368–
370 Latest possible breach. In the case of architects and engineers who are engaged to supervise the work, this may have the effect of continuing an earlier design breach (see the South Australian case of *Edelman* v. *Boehm* and the passages from the judgments quoted in this Supplement *ante* under p. 213) at least until such time as it would cease to be practicable to order a variation or cure the defect, it is submitted.

As to limitation in the case of actions against architects or engineers generally, see the discussion *ante* in this Supplement under p. 123. For the special rules evolved by the Courts in relation to the new economic loss duties owed in tort to owners of houses or other property, see the discussion *ante* in this Supplement under pp. 63–75. For the special limitation considerations arising when invoking indemnity clauses, see the discussion in this Supplement *ante* under p. 306.

370 Fraudulent concealment. *Clark's* case. It seems clear that the judgment was based on the judge's view that the breaches in that case were deliberate, and in the absence of any architect could not be expected to be detected. Subsequent cases show that the breaches must be deliberate—actual knowledge, not constructive, is necessary, though the knowledge of a contractor's responsible supervisor will be sufficient, and a distinction will be made between cases of simple carelessness on the one hand and deliberately scamped work on the other: see *Applegate* v. *Moss* [1971] 1 Q.B. 406 and *King* v. *Victor Parsons* [1973] 1 W.L.R. 29 (C.A.)

SECTION 4. SPECIFIC PERFORMANCE

371– **Specific performance.** See the able discussion of the law on this
373 subject in the outstanding judgment of Mahon J. in *Mayfield
Holdings* v. *Moana Reefs* [1973] 1 N.Z.L.R. 309 at p. 321. Both
Mahon J. in the above case and Helfand J. in *Graham Roberts
Ltd.* v. *Maurbeth Investments Ltd.* [1974] 1 N.Z.W.L.R. 93 held
that specific performance of ordinary building contracts would not
be ordered. An important secondary reason for not ordering the
remedy in ordinary building contract cases is that damages will
afford an adequate remedy.

CHAPTER 6 – ACCEPTANCE AND DEFECTS

SECTION 1. ACCEPTANCE

378 **Add** as illustration (3) the Australian case of *Lamberts* v. *Spry*
illustrated *ante* in this Supplement under p. 59.

379 **Judgment**—i.e. for the money due to the builder. But an anachronistic version of the *res judicata* doctrine appears to create a
difficulty if the employer has previously obtained judgment for
defects and subsequently brings an action for further defects not
previously detected: see in this Supplement *ante* under p. 59.

384 **End of first paragraph** and *Neabel's* case. Add: (and would,
following the *Dutton* case in England in 1972, have succeeded, if
what was involved was a health or safety matter—see the full
discussion *ante* in this Supplement under pp. 63–75).

386 **Defective work during construction.** See the remarks (*obiter*) of
Lord Diplock in *Hosier & Dickinson* v. *Kaye* [1972] 1 W.L.R.,
146 where he suggested that "temporary disconformity" of the
work would not be a breach of contract, if put right promptly on
receipt of an instruction, so that there could not be even nominal
damages for such a breach. It is submitted that this view is not
correct, and ignores the difficulties of correcting errors at a late
stage in building work, and the fact that, unlike many other contracts for work and materials, the work, once incorporated or
fixed, becomes the property of the employer.

SECTION 2. DEFECTS

399 **Final certificate under R.I.B.A. form of contract.** This clause has now been radically amended and will in nearly all cases have no finality—see *infra* in this Supplement under p. 491.

401 **Second paragraph.** A further important class of certificate not mentioned is that found in many contracts associated with the liquidated damages and extension of time clauses, in which the architect makes a final assessment of his combined extensions and certifies that the works as a whole should have been reasonably completed by a certain date. In these contracts the employer's right to recover or deduct liquidated damages is made dependent on this certified date, and not by inference, as in other less precise contracts, from the various extensions granted by him.

CHAPTER 7 – APPROVAL AND CERTIFICATES

SECTION 1. APPROVAL OF WORK

410 **Insert new illustration** (14) and re-number illustration (14) and later illustrations:

> (14) An owner of second-hand machines currently out on hire to various users sold all the machines to a purchaser. The contract of sale provided that the machines were to be supplied with a "Hunt Engineering Certificate," issued by a well-known firm of consulting engineers, to the effect that they had been fully reconditioned to their satisfaction. Both parties thought that there was an objective standard of repair applied by Hunts when giving their certificates. In fact the "certificates" were really reports by Hunts relating to the needs of a particular client (in this case the owner's requirements in relation to his hiring contracts) and the owner's managers had in fact discussed with Hunts the extent to which certain standards might be imposed or modified to suit the owner's requirements. The purchaser sued for damages for defective machines, and the owner pleaded that the certificates were conclusive as to their quality. The purchaser replied that there had been improper interference with the certifier. *Held* by Devlin J., the proffered documents were in reality reports to the owner/seller by Hunts, and were not certificates of quality either in form, substance or intent, nor did they relate to any particular objective standard of quality as the contract contemplated. Accordingly the seller was in breach of contract in failing to provide certificates of the required kind, and the purchaser was entitled to damages for the defects in the machines: *Minister Trust Ltd.* v. *Traps Tractor Trust* [1954] 1 W.L.R. 963.

411 **See** in addition to the illustrated cases, the cases illustrated at pp. 480–483 of the Tenth Edition, and also *Docker* v. *Hyams*, illustrated at p. 415.

Footnote 34. The new (Fifth) I.C.E. Conditions are now satis-factorily drafted from this point of view.

SECTION 2.   APPROVAL BY BUILDING OWNER

413 **Second paragraph.** Implication of reasonableness. No doubt an additional reason, as stated in Halsbury, 3rd edition, Vol. 3, pp. 455–456, is that building work, by becoming attached to the land, becomes irrevocably the property of the owner.

SECTION 3.   APPROVAL BY THIRD PERSON

417– **Traps Tractor case.** Now illustrated in this Supplement *supra*
418 under p. 410.

420 **Insert additional paragraph** at end of subsection (1):

The preceding discussion has centred on whether certificates are or are not conclusive or final in a permanent sense. There is, in fact, a perfectly possible " temporary finality " which the parties may wish to impose until the conclusion of the work, or until arbitration or litigation has finally disposed of the matter. Just such a " temporary finality " was recently thought by the English Courts to attach to interim certificates for payment, following the decision of the Court of Appeal in *Dawnays Ltd.* v. *F. G. Minter Ltd.* [1971] 1 W.L.R. 1205, where employers were held to be precluded from raising matters of over-valuation or defective work as a set-off or defence when sued on these certificates. After a meteoric career producing at least six Court of Appeal decisions to the same effect over a two-year period, the House of Lords in 1973 decisively overruled *Dawnays'* case and the other decisions in *Gilbert-Ash (Northern) Ltd.* v. *Modern Engineering (Bristol) Ltd.* [1974] A.C. 689. See *infra* SECTION 6 (7) " Interim Certificates."

A further possible case where " temporary finality " in the above sense might well be desired by the parties is that of the certificates upon which an employer's right to claim or deduct liquidated damages is often made to depend, particularly since the deduction of sums for this purpose may impose serious if not intolerable financial strains on the contractor: see for this the decision of the Court of Appeal in *Brightside Kilpatrick Engineering Services* v. *Mitchell Construction* [1975] 2 Lloyd's Rep. 493 illustrated in this Supplement *infra* p. 639.

Footnote 63. Add: This view appears to be confirmed (though not directly in issue) in the *Gilbert-Ash* case referred to *supra.*

421 Only a covenant to pay. This statement may be too wide. Simple certification provisions without further wording may only be intended to have a limited or temporary effect for administrative or other special purposes and not to dispose of the parties' ultimate substantive rights: see the reconsideration of the criticisms of *Howden's* and *Errico's* cases *infra* in this Supplement under pp. 424–425.

423 Insert new illustration (13) and re-number (13) and later illustrations.

> (13) Clause 41 of a contract provided for the issue of one-half of the retention monies on the architect's certificate of completion, and for the balance within a certain time thereafter. Clause 42 provided that no sums of money should be considered to be due and owing to the Contractor nor should the Contractor make or enforce any demand on account of any work executed unless the engineer should have certified or recommended the amount to be paid. The certificate of completion was given, but no clause 42 certificate was given (no doubt because of a substantial claim for liquidated damages for delay by the employer which the Court held invalid—see the case illustrated on this at p. 645 of the Tenth Edition and further commented on under the same page in this Supplement *infra*). *Held* by Du Parq J. that notwithstanding the failure of the employer's claim for liquidated damages and the issue of the certificate of completion, the contractor's claim could not, in the absence of the clause 42 certificate, succeed: *Miller* v. *L.C.C.* (1934) 50 T.L.R. 479.

424 Dunlop and Ranken case. See for an expanded criticism of this case *post* under pp. 736–737 in this Supplement.

424– Criticisms of Howden's and Errico's cases. On reconsideration it
425 may be that the absence of any " condition precedent " or " conclusive " or " approval " wording reduces these provisions to mere administrative arrangements for the timing of instalments—it is noteworthy that the cases (1)–(14) at pp. 421–424 nearly all contain more explicit wording than a simple undertaking to pay or entitlement to be paid on certificate. In some cases, too, the main object of the certifying clause may be to form part of the machinery for the exercise by the contractor of a determination clause conditional on non-payment, rather than as a final determination of the employer's substantive liability to pay. The wording needs to be

carefully examined in each case, and the exact relationship of the provision to the remainder of the contract analysed.

433 **The discussion and cases** here do not relate to the special cases of interim certificates, and certificates enabling liquidated damages to be deducted or claimed: see under p. 420 *supra*.

SECTION 4. EFFECT OF ARBITRATION CLAUSE

435 **Operation of arbitration clause**—*i.e.* the effect on the construction of the contract, by virtue of the existence and wording of an arbitration clause, which may indicate an intention that the certificates or decisions in question shall not bind an arbitrator or, if no arbitrator is appointed, the courts if they have become seised of the matter as can easily happen in Anglo-Saxon systems of law.

441 **Absalom's case.** Second line. Delete all after first sentence and substitute: The architect issued an interim certificate which was duly paid, but the contractor claimed that the architect had under-certified, and suspended work, whereupon the employer terminated the contract under a clause empowering him to do so unless there had been a withholding of a certificate to which the contractor was entitled. The arbitrator held that there had been under-certification as claimed, but that it was not of an extent which, under special provisions in the contract limiting the amounts needing to be certified, required the issue of a further certificate, and found for the employer. The contractor applied to set aside the award for an error of law upon its face. *Held* by the House of Lords, that the arbitrator's interpretation of the special provisions had been incorrect, and the contractor had been entitled to a certificate for a larger sum. Since the arbitrator had found that the sum claimed by the contractor from the architect had been correct, he should have revised the architect's certificate himself and awarded that sum, and since there had been a withholding by the architect of a certificate to which the contractor was entitled the employer's termination was invalid: *F. R. Absalom* v. *G.W.* (*London*) *Garden Village Society* (1933) (see this case further illustrated *infra* in this Supplement under p. 490).

Prestige case. Add additional facts:
There was an " open up, revise and review " provision in the arbitration clause. The architect refused to certify because he had

CHAPTER 7 – APPROVAL AND CERTIFICATES

received complaints of defective work from the employer, on which he did not rule but instead referred the contractor to the employer. The Court clearly took the view that in so doing the architect had behaved improperly, but assumed for the purposes of the judgment and on the pleadings that there had been no misconduct. The arbitrator found that no defects existed, but objection was taken that since there was no certificate in the contractor's favour, the arbitrator could do no more than make a declaratory award, but could not actually award money. The Court of Appeal followed *Brodie's* case (surprisingly there is no indication in the report that *Absalom's* case was cited to the Court)—Greer L.J. with some reluctance, and only because he considered himself bound by the *Brodie* and *Neale* decisions (see pp. 438 and 541–543, Tenth Edition). (The *Prestige* and *Neale* cases should be re-numbered and transposed).

442 **After illustration (11) add:** (See also *Ramac* v. *Lesser* [1975] 2 Lloyd's Rep. 430, *post* in this Supplement under p. 639, for the effect of the arbitration clause on the architect's certificate of reasonable completion under clause 22 of the R.I.B.A. contract entitling the employer to deduct liquidated damages).

446 **Add further illustrations:**

(12) By clause 30 (7) of the then current R.I.B.A. contract the architect's final certificate was to be " conclusive evidence in any proceedings under this contract . . . (whether by arbitration or otherwise) " that the works had been properly carried out by the contractor unless notice of arbitration was given before the final certificate by the employer or within 14 days thereafter by the contractor. About the time of practical completion there was a dispute as to the quality of the work and the contractor issued proceedings in the Courts on interim certificates and the employer defended alleging defective work. The employer obtained leave to defend as to a balance of £9,861 after paying £5,000 of the amount claimed. Subsequently the architect issued his final certificate for £2,360, on which the contractor issued a further writ, to which the employer responded with the same defence. Neither side gave notice of arbitration at any stage. *Held* by the House of Lords (Lord Diplock dissenting), that since the employer had not issued a notice of arbitration before the final certificate, it was binding on the Courts in both actions and the employer's defence must fail. There was no need to imply a term, as had been contended, limiting the certificate's effect under clause 30 (7) to subsequent proceedings. *Per* Lord Pearson: to protect his position in the Court proceedings the employer could always issue a purely formal notice of arbitration in such a case: *Hosier and Dickinson* v. *Kaye* [1972] 1 W.L.R. 146.

[*Note*: There are a number of reasons why the above case should be treated as of limited authority. Apart from the obvious difficulties of the decision itself, clause 30 (7) of the R.I.B.A. standard forms has now been altered so as to eliminate (*inter alia*) any such retrospective effect. Secondly, the judgments expressly state that doubts were felt as to the correctness of the decision in the light of a new argument, not previously advanced, which had been put forward by Lord Diplock during argument, but that the majority of the House was not prepared to deal with this argument, since it had not the advantage of full argument and the lower courts' views upon it. In principle the decision seems quite inconsistent with the presumed intention of the parties, and no violence to the language of clause 37 seems involved in construing it in accordance with that intention. Furthermore, the anomalies and practical difficulties created by the decision appear to have been both underestimated and disregarded].

(13) By clause 32 of a civil engineering contract with a Railway Authority, a very wide range of disputes was referred to the Chief Engineer of Railways, whose decision was to be final and conclusive, with a right of appeal on a limited class of matters to "the award order determination or decision" of one of two other officials, "and the arbitrator so appointed shall be the sole arbitrator of the matters . . . referable by way of appeal." By Clause 35 "no suit or action shall be brought . . . to recover any money for or in respect of any breach of contract or for or in respect of any matter arising under this contract unless and until the contractor or the Commissioner shall have obtained a certificate order or award from the Chief Engineer . . . for the amount sued for." The employer purported to determine the contract and the contractor sued for moneys due and damages. The South Australian S.C. (Mitchell J.) had held that clause 32 was invalid as an attempted ouster of the Court's jurisdiction, and that clause 35 was linked with it and shared its fate. *Held* by the High Court of Australia that, whatever the position about clause 32, a provision making a certificate or award a condition precedent to an action was not an ouster of the jurisdiction, and clause 35 was a sufficient answer to the contractor's financial claims. *Held* further, that since there was no act of prevention or interference by the employer, and since certifiers generally must inevitably have to decide matters previously dealt with by themselves and could not be wholly independent, there were no grounds on which the need for the certificate could be dispensed with: *S.A. Railways Commissioner* v. *Egan* (1973) 47 A.L.J.R. 140.

In addition to the cases above, see the decision of the Court of Appeal in *Brightside Kilpatrick* v. *Mitchell Construction* [1975] 2 Lloyd's Rep. 493 illustrated in this Supplement *infra*, p. 639 (architect's certificate a condition precedent to main contractor's right to deduct liquidated damages from sub-contractor).

447 Proposition (e) and footnote 63. See now also *per* Lord Diplock in *Gilbert-Ash* v. *Modern Engineering* (*Bristol*) [1974] A.C. 689 at pp. 719H–720E. And see *Foley* v. *Classique Coaches* [1934] 2 K.B. 1 and *F. & G. Sykes* (*Wessex*) *Ltd.* v. *Fine Fare Ltd.* [1967] 1 Lloyd's

Rep. 53, the reasoning of both of which appears to support this proposition. By analogy in the reverse situation where a remedy conferred specifically on Courts of Record has been extended to arbitrators, see *Chandris* v. *Isbrandtsen Moller* [1951] 1 K.B. 240.

448 Proposition (e). Apart from the presumed intention of the parties, there appear to be two further arguments in support of this proposition. In the first place, if the court is prepared to reject for itself additional powers expressly given to the arbitrator by the parties, it must logically follow that it will reject *restrictions* on those powers placed by the parties—as *e.g.* a certificate which is to bind the arbitrator will not bind the courts, or a time limit or other procedural bar will not bind the courts. Yet it is common for the courts to accept the same restrictions as those placed by the parties on the arbitrator. In the second place, an arbitrator applying powers not granted to the courts would no longer be applying *the law*, which is fundamental to the English concept of arbitration, and the parties if they were so to agree would be genuinely ousting the jurisdiction of the courts, and substituting a system akin to conciliation for deciding their disputes.

SECTION 5. RECOVERY WITHOUT CERTIFICATE

450 Chambers v. Goldthorpe. Now overruled—see *ante* in this Supplement under pp. 165–169.

464 Add second illustration after *Hatrick* case:

> (2) An architect, following a long period of dislocation and strikes for some of which he allowed extensions of time, finally issued a notice of determination under clause 25 of the R.I.B.A. contract in the following terms: " I hereby give you notice under clause 25 (1) . . . that in my opinion you have failed to proceed regularly and diligently with the works and unless within 14 days . . . there is an appreciable improvement in the progress of the works the Council will be entitled to determine your employment. . . ." The contractor contended (*inter alia*) that the principles of natural justice applied to the notice, citing *Hickman* v. *Roberts*, and that they were entitled to be given notice of the " charge " against them, told the substance of the case, and have their representations considered before deciding to issue the notice. *Held* by Megarry J., approving Richmond J.'s judgment in the *Hatrick* case, the rules of natural justice did not apply. The architect's position of independence and his skill was the basis of the parties' safeguards in this type of case: *Twickenham Garden Developments* v. *Hounslow L.B.C.* [1971] Ch. 233 (see this case further

illustrated on other objections to the notice, *post* in this Supplement under p. 689).

SECTION 6. CERTIFICATES

479 **Category (c).** See Chapter 11, p. 639 for certificates relating to extension of time and liquidated damages.

Third paragraph. Definition of certificate. This formulation was approved and cited by Edmund Davies L.J., in *Token Construction* v. *Charlton Estates,* illustrated *infra* under p. 481 (see (1973) 1 B.L.R. at p. 53).

480 **Footnote 89.** Add: See in particular the *Traps Tractor* case, *supra* in this Supplement under p. 410.

481 **Add new illustration:**

(7) By clause 2 (*e*) of a contract the architect was required to make a fair and reasonable extension of time if the works were delayed in one or more of eight listed ways. By clause 16 the employer was entitled to deduct liquidated damages if the architect certified in writing that the works ought reasonably to have been completed by the contract completion date, or any extended completion date, in respect of the period from the certified date until completion. In February 1968 the contractors wrote requesting substantial extensions of time. The work was finished in July 1968. There was no evidence of any further action by the architect until January 1970, when the architect wrote a letter to the employer which stated " I wish to bring to your attention the fact that in accordance with clause 16 of the contract you are entitled to deduct from any payments due to the contractor such sums as are due to you as damages for non-completion. The dates relevant to this calculation are as follows. The original contract completion date was 31.10.67. With 13 weeks' extension of time the adjusted completion date for the contract would have been 30.1.68. The date for the practical completion of the contract was 15.7.68. . . . Details of the 13 week claim for extension of time are being prepared and will be forwarded to you in due course. . . . To summarise, the following are the relevant dates: Contract Completion Date . . . 31st October 1967. Agreed extension of time allowed—13 weeks. This adjusts the Contract Completion date to 30th January 1968. Agreed Practical Completion Dates . . . 15th July 1968." The employer contended that this letter constituted both the extensions of time required to be made under clause 2 (*e*) and the certificate under clause 16. A copy of the letter had been sent to the quantity surveyor but not to the contractor. *Held* by the Court of Appeal, that the contract required the architect, first, to form the necessary opinion following a request under clause 2 (*e*) that it was fair and reasonable to grant an extension and to specify its duration, and then

" make " the extension, not necessarily in writing, and, secondly, to certify in writing as required by clause 16. The letter was ambiguous as to whether or not, and if so what, extension had been granted. Furthermore, following the *Minster Trust* v. *Traps Tractors* case, the letter was not a certificate in " form, substance and intent " since nowhere did it specifically record the architects' opinion that the works ought reasonably to have been completed by a particular date: *Token Construction* v. *Charlton Estates* (1973) 1 B.L.R. 50.

484 Correcting mistakes. Subsequent interim certificates, certainly those of the periodical valuation kind which are nearly universal in the United Kingdom, usually inherently involve the correction of previous certificates, however. Thus they almost invariably are required to represent a retrospective valuation of the whole work done to date, not of the work done since the previous certificate. The reason is partly that the basis of valuation may change as the work progresses—*e.g.* from the value of unfixed materials delivered to site in an earlier month to the later valuation of the same materials incorporated as part of the work—and partly that most valuations are expressly or impliedly only of work *properly* carried out, so that if defects are discovered in a subsequent month the defective work previously allowed will now be disallowed in a later certificate. In the absence of express provision, however, an interim certificate for a particular month may not usually be corrected until the time comes for the next certificate.

491 Employers losing right to question certificate. See, *e.g.* the case of *Hosier and Dickinson* v. *Kaye* under p. 446 of this Supplement.

Chambers v. *Goldthorpe.* Now overruled: see *ante* in this Supplement under pp. 165–169.

The new clause 30 (7) of the R.I.B.A. forms has now been altered, in regard to the quality of materials or workmanship, so that it will be conclusive only in relation to such parts of the work as may be required to be carried out to the architect's satisfaction, and only as to the fact that the architect has been satisfied. Since little if any work is likely to be described in modern contracts in this way, and since, even where this is so, the satisfaction may not in any case be binding on the employer, for practical purposes the certificate is no longer likely to prove a serious obstacle to an employer alleging defective work. The new (Fifth) Edition of the I.C.E. contract has expressly removed all finality from the Maintenance Certificate under that contract, and accords no finality to the new final certificate now provided for in that contract.

492–
494 The views here expressed as to the effect of interim certificates appeared to receive a rude shock when in *Dawnays Ltd.* v. *F. G. Minter Ltd.* [1971] 1 W.L.R. 1205, the Court of Appeal *held* (in a case between main contractor and sub-contractor) that no set-off or defence alleging defective work or over-valuation could be raised against a claim based upon an interim certificate, notwithstanding the presence of a wide-ranging arbitration clause—in effect giving the certificate " temporary finality " until the conclusion of arbitration or litigation at the end of the work. The case was rapidly followed by six further cases reaching the Court of Appeal in a two-year period, all of which confirmed the original *Dawnay's* rule, and extended it to the R.I.B.A. main contract: see the author's article " Set Back to Set-Off " in (1973) 89 L.Q.R. 36, which reviews and criticises all the cases. However the position was restored in July 1973 in *Gilbert-Ash* (*Northern*) *Ltd.* v. *Modern Engineering* (*Bristol*) *Ltd.* [1974] A.C. 689, which overruled all the preceding cases—see the author's Note in (1974) 90 L.Q.R. 21 analysing the precise effect of the *Gilbert-Ash* case—and held that no principle such as that enunciated in *Dawnay's* case existed. It may be stated with confidence, therefore, that in the absence of the clearest express provision, an interim certificate will not debar the employer from raising any matter available as a set-off or counterclaim in proceedings based upon that certificate. In one case with very special facts the House of Lords did hold that such an express intention could be derived from the facts and documents: see *Mottram* v. *Bernard Sunley* [1975] 2 Lloyd's Rep. 197, analysed and commented on in the author's Note in (1975) 91 L.Q.R. 471.

The *Gilbert-Ash* case is primarily concerned with whether the *employer* is bound by an interim certificate. What *Gilbert-Ash* does not finally establish is the question whether an interim certificate is a *condition precedent* to a *builder's* right to sue, if no arbitration clause is present in the contract (all the cases with which *Gilbert-Ash* was concerned contained arbitration clauses) or will at least have " temporary finality " binding on the builder until the end of the work. It is submitted that in old-fashioned contracts with no arbitration clauses interim certification might bind the contractor (*i.e.* it would be a condition precedent to interim payment) unless from the wording the certifying machinery could be regarded as purely administrative (much might also depend on the wording relating to the final certificate itself). See the comment *supra* in this Supplement under pp. 420 and 424–425 modifying earlier criticisms and views about this, and suggesting that perhaps further more explicit wording than a simple provision for payment on certificate might be required, certainly in cases of ultimate liability.

495 Note to Farr's case. There are a number of pointers which indicate that the views here expressed are probably correct (*i.e.* to the effect that under the wording in question contractor's claims disputing valuations can be dealt with in early arbitration). So far as the I.C.E. wording is concerned, it would seem that the matter has in fact been decided in a somewhat different context.

ILLUSTRATION

An architect issued an interim certificate for a total sum of £10,482, leaving a balance of some £900, after previous payments and retention, which was duly paid. The contractor disputed the valuation and contended that the gross sum certified should have been £11,125, and suspended work, whereupon the employer terminated under a clause which empowered him to do so " unless there had been a withholding of a certificate." The arbitrator held that the gross sum certified should have been £11,364, but proceeded to misinterpret a contractual provision about minimum sums to be certified, and consequently held that the contractor was not entitled to a certificate, and therefore that the termination was valid. On an application to set aside the award for an error of law on its face, *held* by the House of Lords, that the arbitrator had misinterpreted the contract, and that based on his finding there had been a withholding of a certificate to which the contractor was entitled, and the termination was accordingly invalid: *Absalom* v. *G.W.* (*London*) *Garden Village Society* [1933] A.C. 592.

So far as the possibly wider wording of the R.I.B.A. contracts is concerned, there are now dicta to the effect that disputes in regard to defects could be referred to early arbitration under the " whether a certificate . . . is not in accordance with these conditions " wording—see *Gilbert-Ash* (*Northern*) *Ltd.* v. *Modern Engineering* (*Bristol*) *Ltd.* [1974] A.C. 689 (at pp. 719H–720A, *per* Lord Diplock), and see also the further dicta in *Burden's* case, referred to in footnote 63, of Lords Radclyffe and Tucker at pp. 1175 and 1181. (In addition, see the South African S.C. decision in *J. C. Dunbar & Sons* (*Pty.*) *Ltd.* v. *Ellgood Properties* [1973] 3 S.A.L.R. 455, where a dispute arose from differing interpretations of the Bills of Quantities, and the Court followed *Farr's* case in allowing early arbitration under a provision permitting " a question of certificate " to be referred before the end of the work).

496 **See** the expanded criticism of the *Dunlop and Ranken* case, *post* under pp. 736–737 in this Supplement.

CHAPTER 8 – VARIATIONS

SECTION 1. GENERALLY

514 **Add further illustrations:**

(13) Clause 2 (*a*) of a contract for power-station foundations stated " This is a Schedule of Rates contract," and that the employer would only be liable to pay for the actual measured quantity of work at the rates in the Schedule whether that should be less or more than the quantity in the Schedule. The quantities were approximately correct but no guarantee was given. The works would also be subject to extras, additions, deductions, alterations, substitutions and omissions as provided for in clauses 10 and 11. Clause 10 conferred power to issue further drawings and details and directions as might be given by the engineer, and clause 11 conferred a wide power to order variations, but placed a limit of 10 per cent. of the contract price, as specially defined, on the total value of omissions. The contract price for this purpose was to be the total value of the work ascertained under clause 2 (*a*) (exclusive of the variations etc. referred to in that clause). The specification stated that the levels and dimensions shown on the drawings were a general indication only and the construction drawings and details might give substantially differing levels and dimensions. The " Schedule of Quantities and Rates " contained the usual four principal columns (unit, quantity, rate and price) found in English Bills of Quantities, with a grossed-up price in a fifth column, and a totalled " contract price " of $6,797,512·38. *Held* by the Court of Appeal of New South Wales, the word " omissions " in clause 11 meant omissions resulting from variations ordered by the engineer and not simple reductions in quantities of earthworks and concrete resulting from the actual levels: *Arcos Industries* v. *Electricity Commission of N.S.W.* [1973] 2 N.S.W.L.R. 186.

[*Note*: This case is interesting because, firstly, it is a classical " Bills of Quantities " or remeasurement contract, despite the use of the " Schedule of Rates " expression (see *ante* in this Supplement under pp. 200–201), and, secondly, because it emphasises the vital distinction between differences in quantities resulting from variations on the one hand and differences arising on remeasurement on the other, which those not familiar with these contracts often find difficult to visualise and understand.]

(14) In a contract containing no express provisions for remeasurement a contractor tendered a lump sum, representing the grossed-up total of the items, estimated quantities, rates and prices in a Schedule required to be priced by all the tendering contractors. This Schedule contained a rate of 15 shillings shown for approximately 49,700 cubic yards of topsoil required to be placed on the finished embankments. The specification provided " If insufficient topsoil to meet the requirements of the Works cannot be obtained within the right of way the engineer may

direct the contractor to obtain topsoil from other approved locations." The 15 shilling rate in the Schedule was grossed-up at the estimated quantities into the tendered lump sum price, but in addition there was a £3 rate, without any estimated quantities and with no grossed-up amount, for importing and placing topsoil from outside the site. In the event there was only 25,000 cubic yards of topsoil available on site, and the contract requirement was also found to be greater than expected at 60,000 cubic yards. *Held* by the High Court of Australia, on its true construction the contractor's lump sum price included for the placing of any amount of topsoil necessary for the contract requirements, if taken from the site without alteration of the contract sum, but in the event of topsoil needing to be imported he was entitled to be paid the £3 rate for whatever quantity needed to be imported, and whether or not it exceeded the total estimated quantities of topsoil: *Commissioner for Main Roads* v. *Reed and Stuart* (1974) 48 A.L.J.R. 641.

[*Note*: This is an interesting example of a "hybrid" lump sum/ remeasurement contract. See the case further illustrated on another point *infra* in this Supplement under p. 533.]

520 Farr case. The language used in the Bills was in fact stronger than that in the Standard Method, and not identical as stated at the end of the paragraph of text—see clause 40 of the S.M.M. " It may be necessary to provide a separate item . . ." See this case now reported in 5 B.L.R. 94, and the remarks of Lords Guest and Pearson there quoted, which doubt whether the Standard Method would be incorporated by clause 57 of the I.C.E. (Fourth Edition) Conditions so as to permit claims for omitted items. (These remarks would not apply to the quite different R.I.B.A. incorporating words in clause 12 of those contracts.)

521 I.C.E. Conditions. Correction of errors. The new (Fifth) Edition of this contract has now adopted the R.I.B.A. clause 13 position and policy—see clause 55 (2) proviso of the Fifth Edition.

521 (d) Schedule of rates contract. Quantities not generally inserted in Schedule. See, however, the *Arcos* case illustrated *supra* in this Supplement under p. 514, and the "hybrid" *Reed and Stuart* case, also under p. 514.

524 Contractors in difficulty. This can also arise as a result of defective work by the contractor.

529 Methods of working. See *ante*, pp. 68–71, 153–155, 324–325 of the Tenth Edition.

SECTION 2. THE POWER TO ORDER VARIATIONS

533 Carr's case. Reference should be to (1953) 27 A.L.J.R. 273 and 89 C.L.R. 327. Tribunal was High Court of Australia.

Add further illustration:

(3) A contract contained an expensive £3 rate for importing and placing topsoil on embankments, and a *lump sum price* for placing all topsoil found within the site (for the contract fully illustrated see illustration (14) *supra* in this Supplement under p. 514). In the event the contract requirements for topsoil were increased over the estimated quantities within the lump sum from 49,700 to 60,000 cubic yards, and only 25,000 cubic yards of topsoil was found to be available on the site. The engineer, being anxious to avoid paying the very profitable £3 rate, omitted the placing of topsoil, to the extent that it was not available on site, under a power to omit in the variation clause, and made arrangements with another contractor for the supply and placing of imported topsoil. *Held* by the High Court of Australia, while the engineer might, by reason of the word " may " in the Specification (which provided " If insufficient topsoil . . . cannot be obtained within the right of way the engineer may direct the contractor to obtain topsoil from other approved locations "), have an option whether to omit some or all of the topsoil requirement altogether, he was, following *Carr* v. *Berriman*, in breach of contract in failing to instruct the contractor to import fill in a case where, as here, he still intended to have the topsoil placed in the quantities required by the contract: *Commissioner for Main Roads* v. *Reed & Stuart Ltd.* (1974) 48 A.L.J.R. 461.

536 Add further illustration:

(2) Clauses 49 (3) and 50 of an I.C.E./F.I.D.I.C.-style civil engineering contract for road works provided that if in the engineer's opinion the contract rates were inapplicable to varied work ordered by him then the contractor should be paid on a cost-plus basis failing agreement. Clause 49 (4) provided that if variations should increase or decrease the value of the total contract amount by more than 20 per cent. then the engineer on proof of loss or damage to the contractor should fix a reasonable price for the variation. Clause 49 (5) provided that no increase in the contract price under 49 (3) or 49 (4) should be made unless as soon after the date of the order as was practicable and in the case of additional work before the commencement of work or as soon thereafter as was practicable notice of intention to claim was given in writing. In September 1969 it was known that the 20 per cent limit had been exceeded. The contractor relied on letters in July 1969 claiming an extension of time, and on December 23, 1969, reserving a general right to claim losses arising from disruption; on a claim for extra costs dated February 1970 which referred back to the December letter; and on a letter from the contractors' lawyers in April 1971 after the work had been completed which first specifically mentioned clause 49 (5). *Held* by the South African Appellate Division (Rumpff A.C.J. and Botha and

Muller JJ.A.) that it was of the utmost importance to both employer and contractor that the machinery should be set in motion during the course of the work and not when the contract was completed: *A. McAlpine & Son* v. *Transvaal Provincial Administration* [1974] 3 S.A.L.R. 506 (further illustrated *infra* in this Supplement under p. 551).

544– **See also** for a case of estoppel, notwithstanding an express require-
545 ment of writing before any change of the specification, the case of *Acme Investments Ltd.* v. *York Structural Steel Ltd.* (1974) 9 N.B.R. (2d) 699 (Appellate Division of New Brunswick S.C.) illustrated *supra* under p. 59.

548 **Work outside the contract.** See also *Salt Lake City* v. *Smith* (1900) 104 Fed.Rep. 457, as to the usual scope of variation clauses, which " is limited by the subject-matter and intention of the parties when it was made, to such modifications of the work contemplated at the time of making the contract as to not radically change the nature or cost of the work or materials required. For all other work and materials required by the alterations the contractors may recover the reasonable value, notwithstanding the agreement."

549 **First paragraph.** Carrying on work without protest. See the *McAlpine* case, further illustrated under p. 551 *infra* in this Supplement, which cited this paragraph and the preceding statements by Lord Cairns and Lord Kenyon. See also *Morrison-Knudsen Co.* v. *B.C. Hydro and Power Authority* (1978) 85 D.L.R. (3d) 186 (Brit.Col. C.A.).

551 **Add further illustrations:**

(3) Tenderers for the construction of a postal terminal were required to exclude the supply and installation of special mechanical handling equipment, on which separate tenders were to be obtained, but to include for overhead expenses supervision and profit. The contract stated " The estimate for the supply and installation is approximately $1,150,000." In the event the con-tractor was instructed by a " Change Order" to place a sub-contract for $2,000,000, and asked for an increase in his own payment. *Held* by the Supreme Court of Canada, the " estimate" was not a mere suggestion or guess, but was a representation intended to be acted on as accurate within 10 per cent in either direction. The contractor had included for supervision, etc. for that amount only, and the difference was properly extra work for which the Crown was liable: *Cana Construction* v. *The Queen* (1973) 37 D.L.R. (3d) 418.

(4) Contractors undertook to build a freeway, the completion period being 30 months. The price was a little over R.4,800,000

including a provisional amount of R.300,000. The work at contract prices increased to over R.6,239,000 plus claims of approximately R.500,000. After the work was finished the contractor was ultimately paid R.6,504,000. The contractors alleged that they had received a very large number of alterations, some of which caused disruption. Although they agreed that the individual alterations were within the scope of the contract, they said the cumulative effect was such that the original contract lapsed and a new contract came into existence by conduct, in terms of which they were entitled to fair remuneration for all work done. They argued that the contract could lapse after completion when the whole work could be assessed, since they were compelled to comply with the engineer's instructions. *Held* by the Appellate Division of South Africa, while at the outset or during its execution a contractor might receive instructions which could not be regarded as falling within the original contract, and might be entitled to fair remuneration under a separate tacit agreement, it must depend on the facts. Here the parties never acted on this basis before completion (or even after completion, when the contractor continued to claim under the contract for a further year). However, no real evidence existed that the road as constructed was not substantially the same as the road contracted for: *A. MacAlpine & Son* v. *Transvaal Provincial Administration* (1974) 3 S.A.L.R. 506.

[See also for an analogous recent decision *Morrison-Knudsen Co.* v. *B.C. Hydro and Power Authority* (1978) 85 D.L.R. (3d) 186, (B.C., C.A.)].

SECTION 3. VALUATION OF AND PAYMENT FOR
EXTRAS AND VARIATIONS

556 Preliminary Items. It is the failure of the Standard Methods of Measurement to analyse or define with any precision the items which should be billed in this way in the classical Bill forms of contract, coupled with the failure of the two industries to achieve any standardised practice on the matter in either Bills of Quantities or Schedules of Rates, which deprives these documents of any real precision when used either for pricing variations or for remeasuring contract work—see the author's article on " The Use of Bills of Quantities in Civil Engineering and Building Contracts " in the *Journal of Maritime Law and Commerce,* Washington D.C., Vol. 6, No. 3 (April 1975). This is compounded, as there pointed out, by the willingness of architects, engineers and arbitrators to accept the right of the contractor to allocate items of expenditure either to preliminary items or to construction-process items, or partly to one and partly the other, and by the absence of any contractual provisions in the United Kingdom standard forms requiring a make-up of his prices to be furnished by the successful tenderer prior to commencement of work. All this is a direct encouragement to claims based on internal pricing arguments tailored to suit such changes in quantities as may ultimately occur.

An attempt at reform has now been made in the "Method Related Charges" definitions and machinery in the new (1976) Civil Engineering Standard Method ("C.E.S.M.M.") in England, which has at least differentiated between preliminary items unaffected by the quantity of work or time (true preliminary items, it is submitted) and those likely to be affected by the quantity or kind of work to be carried out: see Section 7 of C.E.S.M.M. and the separate categories of "Method-Related," "Time-Related" and "Fixed" Charges there defined but this scheme seems complicated and in any event compliance appears to be left to the discretion of the contractor when pricing the contract, of which it seems optimistic to suppose that he will avail himself.

558 **Add new paragraph at end of Section 3:**

Civil engineering contracts outside the United Kingdom not infrequently contain an express limit on the total value of work which may be ordered by way of variation, whether of addition or omission or both, often expressed as a percentage of the contract sum, usually by providing for additional compensation if the limit is exceeded. Such provisions are rarely well drafted, and in particular do not usually exhibit any understanding or foresight as to their administration or operation in practice (or indeed as to whether the contractor is not already adequately protected by the existing provisions for valuing variations). Thus where, as is usual, the limit is on the *net* value of increases or decreases, it may not be possible to tell for certain until the end of the work whether the provision will be activated at all. Again, the precise sum against which the percentage is to be calculated may not always be made clear—as, *e.g.* the original contract sum, or that sum as increased by fluctuations clauses, or other provisions not necessarily concerned with the quantity of work, but which may themselves have affected the value of the variations.

ILLUSTRATION

By clause 11 of a contract for the construction of power station foundations (illustration (13) *supra* in this Supplement under p. 514) the variation clause provided that the total value of omissions of the works should not exceed 10 per cent of the contract price. For this purpose the "contract price" was to be the total value of the work ascertained in accordance with the remeasurement clause 2 (*a*) " exclusive of the value of the deductions . . . and omissions referred to in clause 2 (*a*)." Clause 2 (*a*), after providing for remeasurement in accordance with the actual quantities provided " The works will also be subject to extras, additions, deductions, alterations, substitutions and omissions (*inter alia*) as provided for in clauses 10 and 11." In the event, due to the actual levels, the quantities of earthworks and foundations required by the final construction drawings were substantially reduced. The contractor contended that since the reductions exceeded 10 per cent of the grossed-up contract sum of $797,512.38, his approval was required and he was entitled to compensation. *Held* by the Court of Appeal of New South Wales, overruling the trial judge, that for the purpose of clause 11 the word " omissions " connoted omissions resulting from variations or alterations ordered by the engineer, and not simply reductions in quantities of earthworks and concreting resulting from the actual levels. Furthermore, the 10 per cent must be calculated not on the accepted tender price but on the ultimate remeasured price, in spite of the serious practical difficulties, since the contractor might not know whether he was in a position to withhold approval during the currency of the contract: *Arcos Industries* v. *Electricity Commission of N.S.W.* (1973) 2 N.S.W.L.R. 186.

[See also for an example of this type of provision and of the attitude towards notices of claim under such a provision, *McAlpine's* case illustrated *supra* in this Supplement under p. 551.]

CHAPTER 9 – PRICE AND DAMAGES
SECTION 1. PRICE

564– **Remeasurement.** See also the discussion in this Supplement *supra*
566 under p. 556.

566 **Labour fluctuations clauses.** See also *William Sindall* v. *N.W. Thames Regional Health Authority* [1977] I.C.R. 294, where the House of Lords held that payments made under contractual bonus schemes conforming in all respects with the recommendations in the rules of the United Kingdom National Joint Council (which advocated their use wherever possible), and by which payments were made in accordance with a formula based on current standard time wage-rates, were, nevertheless, not " rates of wages and other emoluments and expenses *payable* in accordance with the rules " since the rules did not compel but only encouraged the payments. (With respect this seems a doubtful decision as a matter of simple interpretation of the word " payable," though binding, of course, in England.) See also *Leighton Contractors* v. *Melbourne etc.*

Board of Works [1975] V.R. 555 ("minimum rates of wages" includes overtime and shift rates as well as plain time).

567 **Second paragraph.** See now the elegant and well-drafted index-based materials clause in use with the I.C.E. Conditions in England, which avoids all anomalies and requires for its effective operation only a reliable series of materials indices, fortunately available in the United Kingdom.

568 **Peak Construction case.** The reference now is (1971) 69 L.G.R. 1, and the case is clearly Court of Appeal authority in England for the proposition that the fluctuation payments will continue to be recoverable by the contractor (or to benefit the employer) during the period of delay if a liquidated damages clause is present in the contract—see particularly *per* Edmund Davies L.J. at p. 15.

571 **Percentage for profit.** See the interesting examination of United Kingdom Government practice on this in Turpin on *Government Contracts*, at pp. 176–178, and 188–192. There are many cases in United States jurisdictions as to what can be charged for as " cost " and what (*e.g.* overheads and superintendence) should be in the percentage—see Am.Jur., Vol. 13 (2d) para. 20.

573 **The United Kingdom standard forms** now have optional clauses for payment for materials not yet delivered to the site.

574 **First paragraph.** See now the further authority and dicta on this point *ante* in this Supplement under p. 495.

Footnote 37. Add: and *per* Lords Radclyffe and Tucker at pp. 1175 and 1181. See also *Absalom's* case and the *Gilbert-Ash dicta supra* under p. 495.

575 **Second paragraph.** Add at end: Indeed refusal by an arbitrator to award interest when sufficient facts are before him will be technical misconduct—*per* Kerr J. in *Van Der Zijden Wildhandel NV* v. *Tucker & Cross* [1976] 1 Lloyd's Rep. 341.

575 **Footnote 44a.** Add: and see *L. & O. Freighters* v. *Timber Shipping* [1971] 1 Q.B. 268 C.A.

577 **Footnote 48a.** Add: and see *FMC Meat Co. Ltd.* v. *Fairfield Cold Stores* [1971] 2 Lloyd's Rep. 221.

SECTION 2. DAMAGES

582 Duty to mitigate. The poverty or financial stringencies of building owners if their project is seriously delayed or serious structural defects develop may well mean that they may have difficulty in making arrangements to complete the work at once. If so, the true view is that they will not be prejudiced because, in considering whether they have failed to mitigate their damage, it will be difficult to show that they have acted unreasonably—see *Bevan Investments* v. *Blackhall and Struthers* (*No.* 2) [1973] 2 N.Z.L.R. 45 at p. 71 (Beattie J.), illustrated *infra*.

584 Add further illustrations:

(9) A sports centre under construction was delayed while the structural design was changed so that the building would be safe. It was necessary to change the designs and incur additional expense, and the owner found difficulty in making immediate financial arrangements to cover the expense, though he at no stage abandoned the intention to do so. The architect and consulting structural engineer were found liable in contract and tort respectively. *Held* by the S.C. of New Zealand (Beattie J.) following the *Cooke, Bellgrove, Harbutt* and *East Ham* cases, that the measure of damage was the amount required to rectify the defects and provide the plaintiff with an equivalent building on its land substantially in accordance with the contract. The plaintiff in delaying resumption of work through financial stringency had not acted unreasonably, and in the circumstances the cost of rebuilding should be assessed at the date of the trial: *Bevan Investments* v. *Blackhall Struthers* [1973] 2 N.Z.L.R. 45.

[*Note*: See also *Radford* v. *De Froberville* [1978] 1 All E.R. 33, a decision of Oliver J., which adopted precisely the same reasoning in a case of breach of a covenant to build. The *Bevan* case has been affirmed on appeal on damages in the N.Z. Court of Appeal in 1977, and the judgment of Richmond P., is of outstanding importance—see [1978] 2 N.Z.L.R. 97.]

(10) Architects negligently employed concrete slab foundations on fill land when they should have used piles. The defects were so serious that demolition and rebuilding was necessary. *Held* by the Court of Appeal of New South Wales, and distinguishing *Bellgrove's* case, the measure of damage was the cost of rebuilding less a credit for the additional cost of a piled design, on the basis that this was not a contract to produce a result for a price, but to give a skilful design: *Auburn M.C.* v. *ARC Engineering Ltd.* [1973] 1 N.S.W.L.R. 513.

[*Note*: Doubts as to the reasoning underlying this decision have been persuasively expressed in the New Zealand Court of Appeal in their as yet unreported judgments in July 1977 in the *Bevan* case. See also the article in 48 A.L.J. 215 commenting on the *Auburn* case.]

587 Illustrations: See also the *Bevan* and *Auburn* cases illustrated *supra* under p. 584.

588 Cost of reinstatement as measure of damage. See also *Acme Investments Ltd.* v. *York Structural Steel Ltd.* (1974) 9 N.B.R. (2d) 699 (New Brunswick S.C. Appellate Division), illustrated *ante* in this Supplement under p. 288.

591 First sentence. This sentence was doubted, if it meant a date *after* the trial, by Beattie J. in the New Zealand case of *Bevan Investment* v. *Blackhall and Struthers (No. 2)* illustrated *supra* under p. 584. While admittedly this would be rare, and it was certainly not intended or contemplated by the sentence in the Tenth Edition, there are in fact cases imaginable where a future date, with a corresponding allowance for inflation, might be reasonable, *e.g.* on fill land, where it is frequently desirable to wait a year or two to allow residual settlement to take place before undertaking further work.

Last sentence and succeeding paragraphs on p. 592: Effect of internal inflation. This passage on the need for a change in the attitude of the Courts in regard to the effect of internal domestic inflation on damages was referred to (*obiter*) with approval by Richmond P. in the New Zealand Court of Appeal in the *Bevan* case, now reported in [1978] 2 N.Z.L.R. 97. See also Feldman and Libling on " Inflation and Duty to Mitigate " (1979) 95 L.Q.R. 270 where the same views are powerfully developed.

599 Capital profits percentages. See also Turpin on *Government Contracts* at pp. 176–178 and 188–192 where percentages allowed by United Kingdom Government departments on cost plus contracts (where, importantly, no risk is involved) of 8 per cent capital employed and 4 per cent on cost are mentioned. Apart from the risk element, these may not, however, be appropriate to building and civil engineering contracts and they also appear to refer to the period before inflation in the U.K. rose into double figures.

601 Loss of productivity. There is, however, no hard and fast rule, and the following Canadian case illustrates the difficulties.

ILLUSTRATION

A contractor undertook to lay track and do the top-ballasting for a railway. A connecting line was to be built between the contractor's line and the owner's existing railway to enable the contractor to get his machinery to the site. There was delay on the owner's part in constructing the connection. As a result the contractor had to start from the centre of his line, and use high-way transportation in place of two locomotives and 10 dumper cars belonging to the owner. There were also delays caused by other contractors employed by the owner. The contractor had sought an extra of 25 cents per ton of ballasting as compensation and so claimed before the trial judge, who awarded $111,577 damages for lack of agreed access and other contractors' delays, based upon the difference between the contract price and a notional contract price had they known of the adverse circumstances in advance. The Court of Appeal reduced this to $55,000. *Held* by the Supreme Court of Canada, there being no evidence that the sum claimed was unreasonable, and when proof of the actual additional costs was difficult, it was proper to use the trial judge's basis: *Penvidic Contracting Co.* v. *International Nickel of Canada* (1975) 53 D.L.R. (3d) 748.

602 Lodder v. Slowey. Though there is no doubt as to the respectability and authority of this decision, and while the same perhaps rather anachronistic rule has been applied in many United States jurisdictions, it may be pointed out that it seems to have little to support it in logic, save a somewhat legalistic and artificial view of the nature of rescission for fundamental breach. It may be doubted if this view in fact would be formed or accepted *de novo* at the present day—and indeed the decision of the House of Lords in *Heyman* v. *Darwins* [1942] A.C. 456 (see the comment thereon *ante* Chap. 5, p. 346 in the Tenth Edition) would suggest that the earlier view may no longer obtain. On principle there seems no reason why a fundamental breach by one party only to the contract should be, in effect, visited with a penalty in the shape of a financial liability greater than the damage actually suffered by the innocent party. See also the judgments of the Court of Appeal of British Columbia in *Morrison-Knudsen Co.* v. *B.C. Hydro and Power Authority* (1978) 85 D.C.R. (3d) 186.

603 Optimistic programmes. These contentions of contractors are almost invariably incorrect. Only if the terms of the contractual provision or other arrangement had the effect of substituting the programme dates for the contract dates for *all* purposes (including advancing the completion dates on which damages for delay depend) could there be any force in such a contention. (Employers under building and engineering contracts, incidentally, rarely if ever have a right to call for *acceleration* of the work.)

603 " Direct loss or damage." See for a further case on this *A. & B. Taxis* v. *Secretary of State for Air* [1922] 2 K.B. 328 (expression includes consequential loss or damage). See also *Croudace Construction Ltd.* v. *Cawoods Concrete Products* (1978) 8 B.L.R. 20 (C.A.).

Add new paragraph entitled: (g) Double recovery of damage.

It is a commonplace of building and civil engineering contracts that a plaintiff may have separate causes of action against two different defendants in respect of the same damage—the classical example being the employer who may have a cause of action for defective work against the builder and for negligent supervision against the architect. In such cases there is no obligation to elect to sue one rather than the other, and the liability of another person for the same damage can only be a defence if and to the extent that the plaintiff may already have " realised " his damage against that other person (*i.e.* by payment or execution of a judgment or award). Similarly, mere judgment or award obtained against another, either in the same or separate proceedings, will not be a defence to proceedings to enforce the judgment or upon execution. (See, *e.g. Campbell Flour Mills* v. *Bowes and Ellis* [1914] 32 O.L.R. 270 (Ontario) where an employer sued an architect and contractor for defective materials and was held not bound to elect. It has been a lacuna in English law that while *tortfeasors* in respect of the same damage had a statutory right of contribution *inter se*, no such right exists in favour of or against a person who is liable in contract—see the ingenious but it is submitted doubtful device adopted by a defendant contractor to overcome this difficulty in *City of Prince Albert* v. *Underwood McLellan* (1969) 3 D.L.R. (3d) 385, illustrated *supra* in this Supplement under p. 153. See now, however, the Civil Liability Contribution Act 1978 which as from 1979 will confer such a right, and which is commented on shortly *ante* under pp. 306–310 in the Supplement.

CHAPTER 10 – TIME FOR PERFORMANCE

604 **Carr's case.** Reference should be (1953) 27 A.L.J.R. 273 and 89 C.L.R. 327.

604, and 609– 612 **Time of essence justifying rescission.** By virtue of their long-term character, delayed building and civil engineering projects are likely to reach crisis-point long before the completion date, so that a word of warning should perhaps be given that much of the discussion under this head will be academic, the vast majority of delayed contracts being terminated before completion under express or implied provisions for due expedition in carrying out the work. An implied term for due expedition (which it is submitted exists in all such contracts, see *infra* in the Tenth Edition at pp. 609–612) is likely to be a far more important practical remedy in most cases. Suprisingly, there is little or no authority on the point in England, no doubt because on very small informal contracts the completion date, or implied reasonable time for completion, will have expired, so that the expired completion date, coupled with notice, was a practical and obvious remedy for a building owner's advisers trained in the conveyancing tradition. On the other hand, in larger projects express terms for due expedition and termination for failure to maintain progress were invariably present in the contracts, and so an equally obvious remedy. The great importance of the implied term may lie in saving a technically invalid determination under an express term, if breach of an implied fundamental term can be shown, and employer's advisers should always if possible rely on such a term in the alternative when drafting documents for a determination, or in any proceedings arising out of the determination.

CHAPTER 11 – PENALTIES AND LIQUIDATED DAMAGES

SECTION 1. CONSTRUCTION AND EFFECT OF CLAUSES

618 First paragraph: limitation of liability rather than liquidated damages. With the increase in the negotiating power of contractors generally in the western world, coupled perhaps with the realisation that the employer, particularly in large projects, may expect to receive substantially higher tendered prices, or even no tenders at all, if he insists upon realistic liquidated damages, there appears to be an increasing tendency for liquidated damages to perform a limiting function, while frequently not changing their apparent designation in the contract (contrast, however, the new (Fifth) I.C.E. Conditions in England, which explicitly recognise this possible alternative role). The law has not yet had time to evolve an approach to this new function in the United Kingdom and Commonwealth, and in such cases much of what is said in this chapter may need reconsideration.

623   Add further illustrations:

(17) A sub-contract contained the words " If the sub-contractor fails to comply with any of the conditions of this sub-contract, the contractor reserves the right to suspend or withhold payment of any monies due or becoming due to the sub-contractor." *Held* by the House of Lords, the provision would entitle the contractor to withhold sums far in excess of the value of his claims, and accordingly was a penalty and unenforceable. *Gilbert-Ash (Northern) Ltd.* v. *Modern Engineering (Bristol) Ltd.* [1974] A.C. 689.

(18) A re-entry clause in a road construction contract entitled the employer to take possession of and use plant owned by the contractor without payment or allowance for fair wear and tear, and retain the plant until payment of all sums ultimately due. *Held* by the High Court of Australia, this provision for use and providing security was not a penalty, in the absence of an absolute transfer of ownership or (*per* Jacobs J.) any indication that the employer would thereby get the contract completed more cheaply than under the original contract provisions. *Forestry Commission* v. *Stefanetto* (1976) 8 A.L.R. 297.

SECTION 2.   RELEASE OF LIQUIDATED DAMAGES

625   In considering the cases, it should also be borne in mind that whereas many nineteenth-century forms of contract required the architect to deal with questions of extension of time and liquidated damages in his payment certificates, the standard forms in England in the present century usually provide for extensions of time, or any other attendant certification in regard to liquidated damages, to be effected separately from the interim or final certificates for payment, so that under the modern forms no inferences can be drawn from the payment certificates as to the architects' decisions or actions in regard to liquidated damages. The object of the modern type of procedure is to give the employer, once the relevant certificate has been obtained, a discretion whether or not, and if so to what extent, to exercise his consequential power of deduction, since in some situations there may be compelling commercial reasons why the employer may not, in his own interest, wish to deduct some or all of the sums due to him until the work is nearer completion.

626   Add at end of text before illustrations:

(and upon which by definition the certifier has been given no power to rule or decide). The attitude to this problem in United States jurisdictions has been mixed—see Am.Jur. Vol. 13 (2d), paras. 49 and 86, but there is now no doubt about the position in England and the Commonwealth jurisdictions. One further powerful consideration showing the English and Commonwealth view to be logically correct is that, as Lord Pearson said in the *Trollope* case (see under p. 633 *infra*), once the contract date is no longer applicable, the reasonable time for completion which must be substituted is not necessarily the same thing as the contract date plus a reasonable extension. However, while there seems no doubt about the position where no applicable ground of extension is stipulated in the contract, the cases which refuse to interpret a ground expressed in very general terms so as to cover acts or omissions of the employer may perhaps now be open to reconsideration in the light of the generally more sympathetic attitude to liquidated damages clauses now to be found both in the English courts and in commerce.

629 **Footnote 53, Dodd v. Churchton. Add:** Approved by Lord Pearson in *Trollope & Colls* v. *N.W. Metropolitan H.B.* [1973] 1 W.L.R. 601.

Murdock v. Luckie. In this case the contract specifically required the architect to grant an extension of time at the time of ordering the extras. The architect in fact considered that the contractor was entitled to the extension, and simply issued a final certificate making no deduction. The employer counterclaimed for liquidated damages arguing that the architect had made no extension of time as required by the contract. This background may help to explain the rather legalistic reasoning of the Court.

631 **Note on Perini Pacific case.** The *Perini* clause was similar, but not identical, to the (Fourth Edition) I.C.E. Conditions then current. However the new (Fifth Edition) I.C.E. Conditions have now greatly increased the expressed grounds for extension of time so as explicitly to cover most forms of employer-prevention or breach.

Add further illustration:

(16) An architect was required to make an extension of time for additions to the works, strikes, *force majeure* "*or other unavoidable circumstances.*" A specialist sub-contractor's faulty work in foundation piling led to a suspension of work and reconsideration of the design, but the local authority employers were guilty of inordinate delay in approving remedial measures first suggested by the sub-contractor, who was prepared to carry them out at once free of charge, and which were later approved and recommended by an independent engineer called in by the

authority. The local authority deducted liquidated damages for the whole period of delay. The main contractor did not dispute this and sought to recover from the sub-contractor (a) the liquidated damages and also (b) payments which would otherwise have been due under a labour fluctuations clause in the main contract, but which related to the period after the extended contract completion date, and which the local authority had for that reason refused to pay. *Held* by the Court of Appeal, (a) following *Holme* v. *Guppy* and *Wells* v. *Army and Navy, etc.*, that since the employer was responsible for a part of the delay, and since no applicable extension of time clause covering the employer's delay existed, the liquidated damages clause could not be invoked, and the employer was left to recover such damages as he could prove flowed from the contractor's breach; (b) that in any event, following *Miller* v. *L.C.C.*, the architect not having been asked to grant and not having in fact granted an extension of time, liquidated damages could not be recovered; and (c) that the employer was bound to pay, on a true interpretation of the fluctuations clause, all increases in wage rates until actual completion. If the basis of the employer's claims for delay was to be changed to the actual damage suffered by him, then the true measure of damage would be the much smaller sum whereby the fluctuations payments under the contract were increased by the delay caused by the sub-contractor compared with what would have been payable under the fluctuations clause but for that delay: *Peak Construction Ltd.* v. *McKinney Foundations Ltd.* (1971) 69 L.G.R. 1.

Footnote 59. Add: See also the comments of Menhennitt J. as to a possible implied term basis for the rule in *Aurel Forras Ltd.* v. *Graham Karp Ltd.* [1975] V.R. 202.

Footnote 64. *Wells* case reference in Hudson's B.C., 4th ed., Vol. 2, should be to p. 346.

632 **Footnote 67.** Reference to approval in the *Perini* case should be to the Court of Appeal of British Columbia (see p. 630, footnote 58 in the Tenth Edition) and not to the Supreme Court of Canada.

633 **First paragraph,** end of subsection (1), add: This statement is, however, made on the assumption that the liquidated damages will exceed or be an over-estimate of actual damages, and not in relation a clause which in reality is intended as a limitation on liability, or in a case where true damages would enable the employer to increase his claim: see the discussion under p. 618 *supra* of this Supplement. Moreover " reasonable time," if substituted in this way on failure of a liquidated damages clause, will not, it should be borne in mind, necessarily be the same as the contract period plus a reasonable extension for the delay caused by the employer:

see *per* Lord Pearson in *Trollope & Colls* v. *N.W. Metropolitan Hospital Board* [1973] 1 W.L.R. 603.

SECTION 3. EXTENSION OF TIME

639 **Two difficulties facing certifiers** when dealing with applications for an extension may be mentioned. First, different causes of delay may overlap, and this will be intellectually troublesome if one is an event justifying an extension and one not; *e.g.* information or access may not be available, but due to culpable delay or an event not justifying an extension, the contractor would not have been able to take advantage of them if they had been. Again, a contractor may be *in advance* of planned progress and an event justifying an extension will only have the effect of his losing that advantage, should some later default occur, but not imperil the actual date. Ideally such an extension need only be given if the contractor later has need of it—*i.e.* by being in culpable delay—see Megarry J.'s view as to the effect of the R.I.B.A. wording in such an eventuality in the *Twickenham* case [1971] Ch. 233 at p. 263. As to events which would otherwise justify an extension occurring during the period of delay, see the discussion *infra* in this Supplement under p. 653.

639 **Second paragraph.** Contents of certificate. Considerable precision of wording will be required by the courts if a document is to be construed as a certificate authorising the deduction of liquidated damages: see the case of *Token Construction Ltd.* v. *Charlton Estates* (1973) 1 B.L.R. 50, illustrated *supra* in this Supplement under p. 481.

Add further illustrations:

(2) A building owner paid £1,000 to the builder, under a final certificate for £11,744 less a simply expressed " contra " for liquidated damages of £10,744, showing a balance of £1,000. The certificate was drawn up by the owner's salaried employee architect. The builder sued for the remaining £10,744. Subsequent to the writ, the architect endeavoured to regularise the position under the R.I.B.A. conditions by issuing an appropriate clause 22 certificate upon which the right to deduct was expressed to depend (by cl. 22 " If the contractor fails to complete by the extended time fixed . . . and the architect certifies in writing that in his opinion the same ought reasonably to have been so completed, then the contractor shall pay or allow . . . and the employer may deduct . . ."). The owner sought to stay the action for arbitration, but the builder objected that at the date when the action commenced there was no dispute between the parties, as required by section 4 of the Arbitration Act 1950, so that no stay could be

granted, though he conceded that if the matter remained in the High Court the owner under the R.S.C. would be entitled to rely on and plead the clause 22 certificate as a defence notwithstanding its issue after the writ. *Held* by Forbes J. that a dispute already existed when the employer disputed the full payment under the final certificate, and also before that as to the adequacy of the extensions of time previously granted. Though a clause 22 certificate might be a condition precedent to recovery of liquidated damages it was not a condition precedent to arbitration, and under the arbitration clause the arbitrator had power to decide the question irrespective of whether or not there had been an architect's certificate under clause 22. Accordingly the action would be stayed: *Ramac* v. *Lesser* [1975] 2 Lloyd's Rep. 430.

(3) In an informally concluded sub-contract with a number of inaccurate references to documents, the Court finally held that the parties had contracted under the terms of the F.A.S.S. " Green Form " of nominated sub-contract, and had agreed a contractual completion date. By clause 8 (*a*) of that form the contractor was not entitled to claim loss or damage for delay by the sub-contractor unless a certificate in writing that the sub-contract works ought reasonably to have been completed within the specified or extended period had been issued by the architect. The architect refused a certificate but the main contractor deducted. *Held* by the Court of Appeal, that in the *Ramac* case the question was merely whether the dispute was one which ought to be arbitrated under the arbitration clause in the R.I.B.A. contract or whether it should be litigated in the courts. Here clause 8 (*a*) amounted to a condition precedent, the architect had refused his certificate, and the sub-contractor must succeed: *Brightside Kilpatrick Engineering Services* v. *Mitchell Construction (1973) Ltd.* [1975] 2 Lloyd's Rep. 493, C.A.

[**Note:** The *ratio decidendi* of this case is unfortunately quite unclear. The arbitration clause in the F.A.S.S. form is in general terms, but does not, unlike the R.I.B.A. forms, specifically confer an " open up, revise, and review " power. The judgments fail to discuss the arbitration clause at all, or to indicate whether, perhaps, it was not regarded as incorporated into the sub-contract, or whether, perhaps, its terms were not sufficiently wide to enable an arbitrator to disregard the clause 8 (*a*) requirement, or whether, perhaps, what was being accorded by the Court was only a *temporary* finality to the architect's refusal of a certificate (so that the main contractor must for the time being pay in full but still be free at the end of the day to recover back his damages in an arbitration). If the arbitration clause was to be regarded as incorporated it seems at least fairly strongly arguable that, if in general terms with no express exclusion of delay claims, it would enable an arbitrator to decide the matter at the end of the day—see Chapter 7, Section 4 of the Tenth Edition—subject to the counter-argument (which should be borne in mind in construing a doubtful contract on this point) that an architect, by reason of his special personal knowledge and periodical presence throughout the work may be better qualified to judge questions of delay than an arbitrator appointed after the event, so that the parties may for these reasons not unreasonably intend his certificate to prevail, whether permanently or temporarily, over the views of an arbitrator or the courts. This is not generally, however, likely to be the subjective intention with the standard forms in England, where the contractor and sub-contractor presence on the negotiating bodies is extremely powerful.]

644– **Some re-consideration of the effect of the A.B.C. and other cases**
645 referred to in the Tenth Edition, *infra*, may be required. In that
case the contractor was apparently taking the point that, if the
extension in question was invalid, this would invalidate the
employer's claim to liquidated damages altogether; whereas Lord
Denning clearly considered that the arbitration clause in the
A.B.C. case, with its " open up review and revise " power, would
enable an arbitrator to review the matter in any event. The existence of an arbitration clause wide enough to enable the certifier's
decision to be reviewed on the merits at the suit of either party will
mean that there is little point in having a contractual time limit on
the certifier's power to extend time, and this may well have
influenced the Court on the question of interpretation more than
is indicated in the judgments. In *Miller* v. *L.C.C.*, on the other
hand, there is no evidence of there having been an arbitration
clause, and in any event the engineer's certification of both extension of time under clause 31 and liquidated damages under clause
37 in that contract was expressed to be final. Moreover, the extension of time under clause 31 was to be *the only compensation* for
lack of information or impediment or obstruction by the employer.
In a situation where extra work was ordered and other delays were
as a fact caused by the employer, it is not surprising that with such
a severe contract Du Parq J. was prepared to hold that the powers
should be exercised in time to enable the contractor to re-arrange
his programme if necessary. Again in *Anderson* v. *Tuapeka C.C.*,
the clause was limited to variations only and read " in the event of
any alterations . . . being required the engineer shall allow such
extension of time as he shall think adequate in consequence thereof
and any sum to be payable by way of damages . . . shall be com-
puted from the expiration of such extended time." There the
contract completion date was November 1897, the principal variation was ordered in September 1897 and the architect's extension
was made in June 1898, seven months before completion in January
1899. In his June 1898 certificate the architect indicated that his
extension was from September 1897 to a date in May 1898, and
authorised the appropriate deductions from the sums certified. The
New Zealand Court of Appeal's reasoning is indicated by the
following statement of Edward J. ([1900] N.Z.L.R. 1 at p. 17):

> "They could not, under that [the employer's] construction,
> know until the final completion of the works whether they
> were incurring any and if so what penalties and they could

not therefore make extraordinary efforts to avoid incurring such penalties as otherwise they might do."

However, it should be noted that the *Miller* case was (*obiter*) purportedly followed by the Court of Appeal in *Peak Construction Ltd.* v. *McKinney Foundations Ltd.* (1971) 69 L.G.R. 1 (illustrated *supra* in this Supplement under p. 631), in a case where no extension at all had been granted but where an arbitration clause did exist.

646   Add further illustration:

> (4) Clause 35.2 of an engineering contract provided " If the engineer be of opinion that the cause of the delay is such as to justify an extension of time . . . the engineer shall grant such extension of time as he thinks fit." Clause 40.1 provided that the contractor might give notice if a variation prevented the contractor from fulfilling any obligation under the contract, the engineer was to give notice of confirmation " forthwith," and if the engineer confirmed the order for the variation the contractor's obligations would be varied. The contract completion date was December 1969. Variations were ordered and claims for extensions sent in up to December 3, 1969. In April 1970 the engineer acknowledged the various letters and suggested a meeting. On April 23, 1970, the engineer wrote purporting to grant extensions and on the same date issued certificates deducting the appropriate liquidated damages. Completion was on May 29, 1970. *Held* by the S.C. of West Australia (Burt J.), (a) that clause 35.2 was not, but clause 40.1 was, a clause which permitted extensions of time for variations; (b) even if clause 35.2 applied, on its true construction an extension of time must be given within a reasonable time and, if not, liquidated damages were not recoverable (*Miller* v. *L.C.C.* cited); (c) in the present case the extension was not granted within a reasonable time under clause 35 or " forthwith " under clause 40: *MacMahon Constructions* v. *Crestwood Estates* [1971] W.A.R. 162.

646   Second paragraph. This may require reconsideration. In the absence of an over-riding arbitration clause or express provision, a reasonable time for this purpose cannot be later than a short interval after the effect of the last matter justifying an extension can be estimated—this is necessary from the employer's point of view as well as the contractor's. (As in other parts of this chapter, the views here expressed proceed on the assumption that the liquidated damages clause is one in reality and not effectively a limitation of liability—see the discussion in this Supplement *supra* under p. 618.)

647 Bonus Provisions and Acceleration of Progress.

It is virtually unheard of for building and engineering contracts to contain a power to order an advance in completion dates (*i.e.* acceleration of work), though provisions containing limited powers to order acceleration of progress sometimes exist for use when the contractor is in culpable delay (see, *e.g.* cl. 46 of the I.C.E. Conditions). Except in a case of default by the contractor, however, no doubtful provision should be so construed, it is submitted, since it may be totally subversive of the economics of the contract.

648 Add new sub-section (7) entitled " Phased Completion."

Phased completion is now contemplated by one United Kingdom standard form (the (Fifth) I.C.E. Condition with its provisions for " Sectional Completion " under cl. 47). In the absence of expressly designed standard provisions the parties frequently make use of ordinary unaltered standard forms without realising the complications likely to result.

ILLUSTRATION

Phase I of a contract using the R.I.B.A. standard forms was to be completed on April 30, 1969, subject to any extensions of time under clause 23. Phase III was to start six months after the certificate of practical completion of Phase I, and be completed by April 30, 1972, subject to extension of time grounds which made no mention of Phase I being completed late as a ground for extension of Phase III. Phase I was delayed by 59 weeks, for which an extension of time for Phase I of 47 weeks was given. This had the effect of reducing the period of construction for Phase III from 30 months to 16 months (on the basis of 59 weeks delay to Phase I). The employers (who could not nominate sub-contractors for Phase III in time, or able to quote, for this greatly reduced period) sought a declaration that the contract period for Phase III was subject to the same extension as that granted for Phase I. A majority of the Court of Appeal held that there was an implied term to this effect. *Held* by the House of Lords, there were four possible formulations of the implied term involving an extension of Phase III equivalent to: (a) those extensions for Phase I which had been due to acts of the employer; (b) the extensions actually certified by the architect for Phase I; (c) those extensions properly allowable for Phase I (*e.g.* by an arbitrator); and (d) the total actual period of delay on Phase I; and that, in view of the various quite different alternatives, no term could be implied. *Per* Lord Dilhorne: he was satisfied the real intention had been to allow 30 months from actual completion of Phase I for completion of Phase III. *Per* Lord Cross of Chelsea; he agreed that the contract without any implied term did not express the parties' real intention: *Trollope & Colls Ltd.* v. *N.W. Metropolitan Hospital Board* [1973] 1 W.L.R. 601.

SECTION 5. POLICY OF LIQUIDATED DAMAGES AND
EXTENSION OF TIME CLAUSES

652 Jarvis case. Reference [1969] 1 W.L.R. 1448 is to C.A. H.L. reference is [1970] 1 W.L.R. 637.

653 One further matter not covered by the vast majority of extension of time clauses is whether they are intended to operate during a period of culpable delay in respect of matters which, but for the contractor being in delay and already liable to liquidated damages, would entitle the contractor to an extension. Careful analysis shows that, if so, additional machinery is required: (a) for certification that, but for the new qualifying event, the works would now be complete (not till this certificate could the pre-existing liability to continue paying liquidated damages properly terminate); and (b) for a further certification that the works should now be complete (assuming that the contractor was guilty of further delay after the new qualifying event) which would revive the liability to pay liquidated damages. This is by no means academic—contractors seek to argue, for instance, that once in culpable delay no variation, for example, can be ordered without invalidating the liquidated damages clause, since no machinery exists to deal with the matter. A well-drafted clause should therefore make provision for further extensions, with machinery similar to that already indicated, at least in respect of those matters for which the employer is responsible—as, *e.g.* variations, late information, or access—as opposed to other matters such as weather or strikes, where no extension need be given since, but for the contractor's own culpable delay, they would not have affected the contract. No U.K. standard form as yet contains any such provision.

CHAPTER 12 – VESTING AND SEIZURE OF
MATERIALS AND PLANT

SECTION 2. EXPRESS PROVISIONS

668 Add further illustration:

(15) A main contract contained a " vesting clause " for plant etc. to become the employer's property, with powers to order its removal, or the substitution of proper plant. The contractor's order to a sub-contractor enclosed a copy of the main contract stating " it must be drawn to your attention that the conditions as laid down in the contract documents must be adhered to at all

times . . . you will be paid on the same basis as [the main contractor]." The engineer under powers to do so ordered the exclusion of the sub-contractor from the project, being dissatisfied with his work, and brought proceedings for an injunction to prevent the sub-contractor removing his plant. *Held* by the High Court of Southern Rhodesia: (a) that the " vesting clause " had not been incorporated into the sub-contract; and (b) only the main contractor could sue upon or enforce the sub-contract: *Triangle Ltd.* v. *John Burrows Ltd.* [1958] 3 S.A.L.R. 811.

678 Sub-section (7). See the *Triangle* case *supra* in this Supplement under p. 668.

CHAPTER 13 – FORFEITURE AND DETERMINATION

SECTION 1. THE GENERAL NATURE OF THE POWER TO FORFEIT OR DETERMINE

681 The Twickenham case: The *Twickenham* appeal was not proceeded with. Megarry J.'s decision was almost immediately criticised in 87 L.Q.R. 309–312, powerfully disapproved and not followed by Mahon J. in New Zealand in 1973, similarly not followed in New South Wales in 1974, and was in fact contemporaneous with a directly contrary decision in Victoria—see *post* in this Supplement under p. 712, where the opposing cases are preferred.

684 Contractor's express rights of determination. The comment should be limited to domestic contracts. International contracts often confer such a power, though usually limited to non-payment by the employer.

689 Add further illustration:

(3) Clause 25 (1) of the R.I.B.A. contract permitted determination following a notice " specifying the default " for (*inter alia*) " failure to proceed regularly and diligently with the works." The architect wrote a letter " I hereby give you notice under clause 25 (1) . . . that in my opinion you have failed to proceed regularly and diligently with the works and unless within 14 days . . . there is an appreciable improvement in the progress of the works the Council will be entitled to determine your employment." The contractor objected that the notice failed to specify the matters relied on in support of the allegations, and also that the words " in my opinion " invalidated the notice, which should have made a factual statement. *Held,* by Megarry J., that the notice was a valid notice. *Twickenham Garden Developments* v. *Hounslow L.B.C.* [1971] Ch. 233.

(See this case further illustrated *ante* in this Supplement under p. 464 for certain other objections to the notice taken by the contractor.)

694– **Construction of clause.** The Anglo-Saxon jurisdictions have
695 traditionally construed strictly the procedural or formal requirements of express provisions for determination.

ILLUSTRATION

A contract provided for an initial notice of default by registered post, and that if the default continued for 14 days, notice ter-minating the contract might be given. The first notice was delivered by hand to the foreman on site, and the second notice was posted a fortnight later, arriving the following day. *Held* by the S.C. of New South Wales (Collins J.): (a) that the require-ment of notice by registered post must be complied with; (b) that the posted notice must as a matter of law be treated as given when posted; so (c) the second notice, having been given on the 14th day after the first, though arriving on the 15th, was invalid, since 14 clear days were required. *Erikson* v. *Whalley* [1971] 1 N.S.W.L.R. 397.

SECTION 3. WRONGFUL FORFEITURE

711 **Lodder v. Slowey.** See, however, the doubts as to the principle in this case expressed *supra* in this Supplement under p. 602, and the recent decision of the British Columbia Court of Appeal in the *Morrison-Knudsen* case there referred to.

712 **The Twickenham Garden case:** This was settled before appeal, and so has not yet been reviewed in England. If correct it would be com-mercially disastrous for employers, either when faced with an intransigent contractor or when desiring to abandon a project on commercial grounds. It is submitted that it was in fact wrongly decided, for a number of compelling reasons.

ILLUSTRATIONS

(1) Progress on a major housing project for a London Borough Council became increasingly delayed, the principal cause being strikes over the implementation of the contractor's bonus scheme. At first the architect granted extensions, but ultimately came to the conclusion, following a resumption of work, that the con-tractors, who were demanding increased contract prices as a condition of continuing work, were not making serious or com-petent efforts to control the labour force or obtain proper productivity, and by letter by registered post served notice under

clause 25 of the R.I.B.A. contract for failure to proceed regularly and diligently with the work. There being no improvement, the Council by notice under the clause determined the contractors' employment. The contractors maintained their security personnel on the site and refused to leave, alleging that the determination was unjustified. The Council brought proceedings for possession and damages, and for an interim injunction, conceding that the issue of the determination would have to be litigated or arbitrated. *Held* by Megarry J., that although the contractors had no right to insist on the employers continuing to perform the contract, the contract was for the execution of specified works on the site during a specified period, and although the contractors did not have a licence coupled with an interest, the contract was at least subject to an implied negative obligation not to revoke the licence except in accordance with the contract during that period, so that without compelling evidence of a valid determination by notice the Court would not grant an injunction compelling the contractors to leave. While the notices were properly given in accordance with the contract it was not possible to decide on conflicting affidavit evidence whether the notices were justified, so that no injunction would be ordered. *Hounslow L.B.C.* v. *Twickenham Garden Developments* [1971] Ch. 233.

[*Note:* (Some of the facts in the first two sentences of the illustration do not appear from the report and are *ex. rel.* the Editor.)
Apart from the overwhelming practical objection that the decision produces a position of legal stalemate, with a contractor in possession unable to insist on being paid and an employer out of possession unable to make arrangements for completion of the project, and apart from the objection of first principle that such a situation could not possibly represent the contract intention, since it deprives any clause for re-entry based on controversial facts of any practical value, and presents the contractor with what is in effect a lien on uncompleted work, the decision is open to the legal criticism that Megarry J. relied heavily on the " ticket " and " theatre " cases in support of his " implied negative term "—but these cases were different from building contracts in a most fundamental sense, since the whole object of the transaction in a " ticket " case is the occupancy of the seat by the ticket-holder for the relevant performance or period, and similarly in a " theatre " case the occupancy of the theatre by the theatre company for the period of their run; whereas the occupancy of the land in a building case is purely secondary to the primary object, which is the construction of a building for the owner by the contractor. Once that object has been effectively terminated (and specific performance cannot be granted of such a contract so as to revive it) the object of the occupancy has disappeared. See the criticism of the case in 87 L.Q.R. 309–312 and the precisely contrary decision at about the same date in Victoria of *Porter* v. *Hannah Builders* [1969] V.R. 673.]

(2) A building owner, on the basis that there had been over-payments and defective work, refused further payments until the defects were remedied. The contractor slowed work to a near standstill, and the owner called in new contractors, but they were denied access. The owner applied for an interim injunction. *Held* by the S.C. of New Zealand (Mahon J.), the licence granted by the building owner was not a licence coupled with an interest; and (not following *Hounslow L.B.C.* v. *Twickenham Garden Developments*) there was no implied covenant not to revoke the licence in breach of contract; even if there was such a negative

covenant, it was of no materiality, since the contractor would indirectly thereby obtain specific performance of the building contract, whereas the building owner could not, so there would be no mutuality. There were two principal objections—the implied licence was not necessary for business efficacy, and a contract of this kind could not be specifically enforced. The implication of a term would bring about an impasse, in which the delay before the contractor could get any further payment would be insurmountable; he would not be able to pay sub-contractors; and the architect's authority to co-operate with the builder would be withdrawn; so that the contractor could gain no benefit from staying on the job. From his point of view it would be better to claim for unpaid work to date and loss of profit, since his only object in any case was completion at a profit, while the owner's was to secure completion in accordance with the plans and specification. Both these objects could be achieved, even if the owner was in breach, if he was free to complete by another builder. Furthermore, a determination might be based on defective work. The *Twickenham* case would compel the building owner, in a disputed case, to stand by and watch his building completed in a defective manner. No contractor or owner would ever agree to such express terms. *Mayfield Holdings* v. *Moana Reef* [1973] 1 N.Z.L.R. 309.

[*Note*: This is, with respect, an outstanding judgment. The examination at pp. 318–319 of the practical reasons why no term should be implied is masterly and convincing. The judgment also contains a most clear and thorough examination of the case law as to licences (at pp. 316 *et seq.*) and as to the availability of specific performance (at p. 321) and mutuality (at p. 323).]

(3) When a warehouse building was near completion for an investment company, disputes arose as to how much was due, and the contractor changed locks on the property to prevent the owner's agent from showing round prospective tenants. After various manoeuvres by the parties attempting to dispossess each other, the owner ultimately secured physical possession and wrote to the contractor that the contract was at an end and he was revoking his licence to enter or remain upon the premises. The owner no longer wished to employ the contractor for the purpose of finishing the work. Both parties had given notice of arbitration. The contractor sought a declaration that the employer was not entitled to revoke his licence, that it had not been revoked, and consequential relief. *Held* by the S.C. of New South Wales, Equity Division (Helsham J.): (a) that while the contractor had a contractual licence subject to an implied negative covenant not to revoke it while the contract was still on foot. this was not (following the *Hounslow L.B.C.* case) coupled with an interest; but (b) that, subject only to interference by equity, the licence was revocable at will; (c) that equity would not order specific performance of an ordinary building contract (as opposed to building-lease type contracts); and (d) that on the assumption that the revocation was wrongful, which would have to be determined in the arbitration, no sufficient reason existed for an injunction, since damages would be a sufficient remedy, and to grant an injunction would be to force the defendant to pay a disputed

claim in advance of the arbitration, or have the building completed by a builder with whom he was in dispute. *Graham Roberts Ltd.* v. *Maurbeth Investments Ltd.* [1974] 1 N.S.W.L.R. 93.

[*Note*: Surprisingly, the report does not indicate that the very similar and recent *Mayfield Holdings* case in New Zealand was cited to the New South Wales Court.]

CHAPTER 14 – ASSIGNMENT

SECTION 1. ASSIGNMENT OF CONTRACTUAL LIABILITIES

718   **Second paragraph.** Printing error in second sentence, which should read: " If this view is correct, then a main contractor's trustee in bankruptcy or liquidator, or a sub-contractor for the whole of the work . . . ."

SECTION 5. ASSIGNMENT OF MONEYS DUE

728–   **In addition to illustrations,** see *Drew* v. *Josolyne* (1887) 18 Q.B.D.
729   590 illustrated *post* in Tenth Edition at p. 795.

729   **Footnote 60.** Add: *Per* Wynn-Parry J. at p. 187 " They represent monies already earned." See also *Monkhouse Ltd.* v. *Premier Windows* [1968] 2 N.S.W.L.R. 664.

730   **Tout & Finch,** *Re* the effectiveness of the *Tout & Finch* type of provision, even where the money is available in the hands of a third party, must now be regarded as at least open to reconsideration in the light of the difficult House of Lords' majority decision in *British Eagle International Airlines* v. *Cie. Nationale Air France* [1975] 2 All E.R. 390. See also *infra* in this Supplement under pp. 770–771.

734   **Prohibition of assignment of contractual rights.** See now *Helstan Securities* v. *Hertfordshire C.C.* [1978] 3 All E.R. 262, where a contractor was prohibited from assigning " the contract . . . *or any benefit or interest therein* " without the written consent of the employer, and Croom-Johnson J. held that an assignment by the contractor of monies due without consent was effectively invalidated by the provision.

736–   **Re-consideration of the cases** makes it clear, it is submitted, that
737   the *Dunlop and Ranken* case in the English Court of Appeal was

736– wrongly decided (except only on one possible view), and that the
737 Alberta Courts in *Sandy's* case were right not to follow it. In the
(cont.) first place, examination of the judgments in *O'Driscoll* v. *Manchester Insurance* [1915] 3 K.B. 499 shows that in upholding
attachment they proceeded on the basis that the sums in question
were in the category of debts already earned but not yet due—
debitum in praesenti, solvendum in futuro—but were faced with the
difficulty that they could not be exactly quantified at the time of the
attachment. This case and *Tapp* v. *Jones* makes it clear that money
not yet due, but already earned, even if unquantifiable, may nevertheless be attached. The cases of *Webb* v. *Stenton* (1883) 11 Q.B.D.
518, and the *Grant Plant Hire* case, are easily distinguished, because
in the *Webb* case no debt existed yet, and might never exist at all,
at the time of attachment, while in the *Grant* case the principal
contract *expressly* provided that in the events which had happened
no further payment need be made (and might well never be made).
(Compare the analogous cases on assignment of retention moneys
of *Drew* v. *Josolyne* (1887) 18 Q.B.D. 590 illustrated at p. 795 of the
Tenth Edition, and *Tout* v. *Finch* [1954] 1 W.L.R. 178, illustrated
at p. 729 of the Tenth Edition.)

Turning to the *Dunlop and Ranken* case, this could only be
justified on the basis that the arbitration clause in the main contract
was disregarded by the Court of Appeal, and that the certificate in
question was held to be a condition precedent to the right to
recover. If the arbitration clause was to be taken into consideration
as part of the sub-contract, *Absalom* v. *G.W.* (*London*) *Garden
Village* (1933) A.C. 592 and *Prestige* v. *Brettell* [1938] 4 All E.R.
346, illustrated at pp. 440–441 of the Tenth Edition (and see *supra*
under those pages) show that the moneys due could be recovered
without a certificate in such a case—see also under p. 495 *supra* in
this Supplement. Even if the Court of Appeal in the *Dunlop* case
was proceeding on the basis that there was no arbitration clause
in the sub-contract, a simple provision for payment on certificate,
without further more specific wording indicating that no sum
should be due without the certificate, may well be insufficient to
make a certificate a condition precedent in the full sense—
see Chapter 7, Section 3 (2) and the discussion in this Supplement
and reconsideration of this subject *supra* under p. 421 and 424–425.
If the certificate is purely administrative, as governing the time
when payment is to take place, or to enable effect to be given to a
determination clause for non-payment, and does not go to liability,

CHAPTER 14 – ASSIGNMENT

then the *debitum in presenti solvendum in futuro* principle will come into play, it is submitted, and the debt can be attached. What renders the *Dunlop and Ranken* case particularly suspect is that it is clear from the judgment of Lord Goddard C.J. that he was equating the sub-contractor's position with that of the main contractor in the main contract, and relying specifically on a note in the *Annual Practice* under O.45, r.1 (now unaltered under 0.49, r.1.8). That note purported to deal with the position under the R.I.B.A. main contract. Yet at the relevant time of the note the main contract had for many years contained an arbitration clause with the wide " open up revise and review " formula in relation to certificates (see the *Absalom* and *Prestige* cases, which were un-doubted authority that the certificate was no longer a condition precedent). Moreover, if the matter is considered in the light of the presumed intention of the parties, it is submitted that a relatively informal incorporation of a main contract certification provision for payment into a sub-contract would not be intended to give the certificate a quite different degree of force in the sub-contract from that obtaining in the main contract, owing to the accident that the sub-contract contained no arbitration clause in sufficiently wide terms.

CHAPTER 15 – SUB-CONTRACTS

SECTION 2. POSITION BETWEEN BUILDING OWNER AND SUB-CONTRACTOR

744–
745
Davies' case. Blain J.'s judgment in this case shows that while the mere act of nomination (*i.e.* the architect's instruction to the main contractor to place his order with the sub-contractor) could not bind the main contractor so as to bring a sub-contract into being (a fairly self-evident proposition having regard, *inter alia*, to the main contractor's express or implied rights of objection), there would have been a binding sub-contract at the moment the main contractor's order reached the sub-contractor but for the intro-duction of the new terms by the main contractor—in other words the architect, in negotiating with the sub-contractor, had effectively produced, as agent for the main contractor, an offer capable of immediate acceptance by him. It would be sufficient for this purpose to show, it is submitted, that in making his original tender the sub-contractor was aware that his work was intended to be the

subject of a nominated sub-contract under a main contract for the project in question.

SECTION 3. BUILDING OWNER AND CONTRACTOR

760 **Third paragraph: Usage for adjustment of P.C. and Provisional Sums.** See the *Tuta Products* case in the High Court of Australia, illustrated *ante* in this Supplement under p. 205.

763 **Architect agent of main contractor.** See also the interesting and typical facts in the Supreme Court of Canada case of *Laminated Structures* v. *Eastern Woodworkers* (1962) 32 D.L.R. (2d) 1, illustrated *ante* in this Supplement under page 287.

764 **Second paragraph: Warranties by sub-contractors.** See the now greatly increased availability of remedies in tort for economic loss, if health or safety factors are involved and, even where they are not, for negligent misrepresentations, discussed *ante* in this Supplement under pp. 63–75.

769 **Add further illustrations:**

(6) A main contractor's order enclosed a copy of the main contract and stated " it must be drawn to your attention that the conditions as laid down in the contract documents must be adhered to at all times . . . you will be paid on the same basis as [the main contractor]." There was a vesting clause over plant, as well as powers of control over it, in the main contract. The engineer under powers to do so ordered the exclusion of the sub-contractor from the site, being dissatisfied with his work, and brought proceedings to prevent the removal of the sub-contractor's plant. *Held* by the H.C. of Southern Rhodesia, the vesting clause was not incorporated into the sub-contract, and in any event only the main contractor could enforce the main contract: *Triangle Ltd.* v. *John Burrows Ltd.* [1958] 3 S.A.L.R. 811.

(7) A main contractor's order was in the following terms " To supply . . . labour plant and machinery . . . in full accordance with the appropriate form for nominated sub-contractors R.I.B.A. 1965 Edition." After hearing evidence (see *ante* in this Supplement under p. 56) and concluding that the reference was intended to be to the F.A.S.S. " Green Form " of sub-contract, *held* by the Court of Appeal, that the words were sufficient to incorporate the arbitration clause of that form into the sub-contract: *Modern Buildings Wales* v. *Limmer and Trinidad Ltd.* [1975] 1 W.L.R. 1281.

(8) A main contractor's order stipulated that the sub-contract documents should comprise (*inter alia*) a Standard Form of

Tender, and Conditions of Contract. After identifying the main (R.I.B.A.) form of contract it then stated "The Conditions applicable to the sub-contract with you shall be those embodied in the R.I.B.A. as above agreement." The Standard Form of Tender stipulated that a sub-contract should be executed and that it should be in terms equivalent to those of the N.F.B.T.E. and F.A.S.S. "Green Form," but no such sub-contract was ever executed. The work was completed and a dispute arose over liquidated damages for delay. *Held* by the Court of Appeal: (a) that the reference to the R.I.B.A. form was only to those clauses in the form relating to nominated sub-contractors; Clause 27 of that form made certain stipulations not inconsistent with the "Green Form"; so the sub-contract should be interpreted in the light of what the parties would have agreed in a formal sub-contract using that Form, had they executed it; and (b) that a completion date for the sub-contract, subsequently agreed but never formally entered into the Appendix of a Green Form, which had never been finally completed, could be treated as though inserted in the Appendix: *Brightside Kilpatrick Engineering Services* v. *Mitchell Construction* [1975] 2 Lloyd's Rep. 493.

Add at end of last paragraph: " I . . . accept that when one comes to read the head contract adapted *mutatis mutandis* in this way . . . many of its clauses are really quite inappropriate and incapable of being given a sensible effect "—*per* Buckley L.J. in the *Brightside* case, *supra,* at p. 496.

SECTION 5. PAYMENT OF SUB-CONTRACTOR DIRECT

770–
771
Effectiveness of a power to pay direct. It should be appreciated that the effectiveness of a power to pay direct will primarily depend upon the domestic law of insolvency, which is usually, of course, statutory as in England. Thus under sections 181 and 182 of the South African Companies Act of 1926, payments direct made after the liquidation pursuant to a contractual provision will not be permitted—see *Administrator Natal* v. *Magill Grant and Nell* [1969] 1 S.A.L.R. 660. Under New South Wales law, however, it is permissible—see *Monkhouse Ltd.* v. *Premier Windows* (1968) 69 S.R. (N.S.W.) 429, which followed *Tout & Finch* expressly. It seems possible, moreover, that, even in England, such a payment after *an insolvency* might, in the case of a company liquidation, infringe section 302 of the Companies Act 1948 (which is the definitive section providing for the payment of classes of creditors *pari passu* upon a liquidation): see the difficult majority decision of the House of Lords in *British Eagle International Airlines* v. *Cie. Nationale Air France* [1975] 2 All E.R. 390 which, while

perhaps distinguishable on the facts, would logically seem to apply in such a situation.

772 The I.C.E. (Fifth Edition) Conditions are now in this respect identical with the R.I.B.A. conditions—see clause 59C.

See also for the extreme complication of a provision for payment direct upon a termination of the main contract, compounded by the use of special bond monies for that purpose, the Australian cases of *Wood Hall Ltd.* v. *Pipeline Authority* (S.C. of N.S.W., April 19, 1977, Eq. No. 320/77) and *Jamison* v. *Mainline Constructions* (1977) (C.A. of N.S.W., C.A. No. 95 of 1976).

CHAPTER 16 – BANKRUPTCY AND LIQUIDATION

SECTION 5. INSOLVENCY OF BUILDER

792 Payment direct of sub-contractors. See for the position as to this in South Africa and New South Wales *supra* in this Supplement under pp. 770–771. See also the difficulties of application of the special power of payment direct in the Australian cases referred to under p. 772, *supra* in this Supplement.

SECTION 7. PRIORITY BETWEEN TRUSTEE AND OTHER INTERESTS

795 Add illustration:

(4) A theatrical costumier assigned all monies due under an agreement whereby for £40 per week she had agreed to supply and keep in repair the dresses for a ballet company. She subsequently went bankrupt. *Held* by the Court of Appeal, following *Ex p. Nichols,* that the assignment did not bind the trustee in regard to sums earned under the agreement following the date of the bankruptcy: *Wilmot* v. *Alton* [1897] 1 Q.B. 17.

Footnote 81. Reference to *Tout & Finch* should be to pp. 187–189 of the report of that case.

CHAPTER 17 – GUARANTEE AND SURETIES

SECTION 1. GUARANTEES AND BONDS RELATING TO BUILDING CONTRACTS

797 Bonds have become extremely popular with foreign governments in international contracts. Performance bonds of 50 per cent or

100 per cent of the contract price are commonplace in the United States, but 10 per cent is the invariable limit in domestic contracts in the United Kingdom.

In addition to Performance bonds, Bid bonds (at the pre-tender stage), and Advance Payments bonds (for due repayment as the work proceeds of advance payments made to secure plant or expensive equipment or for financing purposes) have become common in international contracts. In addition, bonds conditional, not on due performance or payment, but on mere demand without proof of any default or liability of the debtor, have recently become popular with foreign governments who do not seem aware of the additional cost to their contracts likely to result from their use. The English courts have, as might be expected, lost little time in evolving the general rule that in any case of ambiguity a bond will not be construed so as to be enforceable without proof of default in the discharge of the bonded obligation—see Donaldson J.'s decision in *General Surety & Guarantee Co.* v. *Frances Parker Ltd.* (1977) 6 B.L.R. 16 and of the English Court of Appeal in *Edward Owen* v. *Barclay's International Ltd.* [1978] Q.B. 159; (1977) 6 B.L.R. 1. See also the special Australian provision for a bond as an alternative to retention monies, which was held to be conditional on the liability of the contractor to the employer, though on its face expressed to be payable on demand, in *Jamison* v. *Mainline Constructions* (1977) (C.A. of N.S.W., C.A. No. 95 of 1976). See also *Wood Hall Ltd.* v. *Pipeline Authority* referred to *supra* under p. 772 in this Supplement.

SECTION 2. ESSENTIAL REQUIREMENTS AND DURATION

799 Distinction between guarantee and indemnity. The actual words used, such as " guarantee " or " indemnity " are not conclusive and will yield to the sense of the transaction—see *Western Credit Ltd.* v. *Alberry* [1964] 1 W.L.R. 945 (C.A. distinguishing *Yeoman Credit Ltd.* v. *Latter* [1961] 1 W.L.R. 828).

CHAPTER 18 – ARBITRATION

SECTION 1. WHAT IS AN ARBITRATION AGREEMENT

818 Arbitration. Some preliminary observations may be desirable for the benefit of readers not familiar with the English concept of arbitration.

It is perhaps not sufficiently appreciated that the form of the English Arbitration Acts is dictated by the fact that, prior to statutory intervention, the ordinary law of contract meant that any arbitration agreement was, for all practical purposes, unenforceable. This was because, at any time before publication of the award (when a contractual right to enforce the award would undoubtedly arise), either party could unilaterally repudiate the agreement and revoke the arbitrator's authority, thereby depriving any subsequent award of any contractual or other force. On such a repudiation the other party would, of course, be left with a remedy in damages but, in the absence of sufficiently compelling (and frank) evidence as to the superiority, from the complaining party's point of view, of an arbitrator as a tribunal by comparison with the courts (of which, not surprisingly, there is no record in the cases) such an action could only give rise to nominal damages under English law. The fundamental statutory intervention in the nineteenth century, therefore, was designed, while leaving room for a discretion, to render arbitration agreements in effect specifically enforceable, subject to the discretion, against an unwilling party. This was achieved by the two intimately connected sections 1 and 4 of the 1950 Act and the corresponding sections of earlier legislation since the nineteenth century.

Section 1 provided in general terms that the authority of an arbitrator appointed under an arbitration agreement should be irrevocable without the leave of the courts. Section 4 dealt with one of the commonest oblique methods of revoking arbitration agreements, by providing for actions commenced in the courts in a matter already covered by an arbitration agreement to be subject to a discretionary power of the courts to stay the action, and in consequence to force the plaintiff to arbitration. The discretionary power of the courts to revoke under section 1, or to stay under section 4, thus enables the courts to decide, in the last resort, which tribunal shall deal with any particular matter, and notwithstanding which tribunal may be originally seised of the matter. This historical background, and the interdependent relationship of the two sections, is the fundamental basis of the law of arbitration in the English legal system and in other systems based upon it, and an understanding of this will greatly facilitate an understanding of the law and of the Arbitration Acts. The principal feature of the English system is the control over it exercised by the courts, principally through these two sections, but also through

818
(cont.) the Case Stated procedure which, once arbitrations have been started, enables errors of law made by arbitrators in their awards to be corrected, and questions of law to be answered, if necessary in advance of the award itself. It has always been an essential feature of the English system that the arbitrator must be governed by and apply the law, and not by any private ideas of fairness or conciliation. If the parties endeavoured to clothe him with such powers the agreement would cease to be an arbitration agreement under English law. Thus the courts have always been free to set aside an award which discloses an error of law on its face, and it is significant that, where Case Stated is concerned, section 21 of the Act is one of the few mandatory sections in the Act—most of the Act is made to apply by way of an implied term in the arbitration agreement to be applicable only in the absence of any contrary intention expressed in the agreement. The Act is exclusively, and essentially, therefore, concerned with matters of procedure, as is the English law of arbitration itself, and assumes and requires that arbitrators will apply and be bound by the law. There is in fact a widespread and quite unfounded belief in the industry and among arbitrators that they enjoy some sort of special discretion not shared by judges, and indeed that this is their principal *raison d'être*.

Finally, it may be desirable to point out certain *lacunae* in the present law:

(a) The precise purpose and scope of interim awards under section 14 is not defined or explained, and remains obscure.

(b) While nearly all the more important High Court procedural and interlocutory powers are made available under section 12, no machinery for payment into court—a most valuable feature of the English legal system—has been made available—this has led to the privately invented device of the " sealed offer."

(c) The arbitrator's powers to enforce interlocutory orders and directions against a recalcitrant party are not defined with any precision, and are probably inadequate.

(d) While for limitation purposes a notice requiring arbitration is the equivalent of issuing a writ (s. 27 (3) of the Limitation Act 1939) no provision is made for the very common situation where an action is started by writ but subsequently stayed—if so the plaintiff loses the benefit of the date of the writ, which is anomalous. See as an example *County and District Properties* v. *Jenner,* illustrated *infra* in this Supplement under p. 841.

(e) Third party proceedings generally, whether arbitration is involved or not, do not have the benefit of the original writ, unlike a counterclaiming defendant. Nor is there any third party machinery available in arbitrations, except by agreement.

COMPARATIVE LAW OF ARBITRATION

It may also be desirable to give some general indication of the position under other legal systems. The Anglo-Saxon view of arbitrators as being in all cases obliged to decide according to the law appears to be limited to the English and certain Commonwealth or ex-Commonwealth jurisdictions, and to some states in the United States. A second and larger group of nations treat arbitration as subject to varying degrees of control to ensure that arbitrators' decisions accord with the law, but only if the parties so indicate in their arbitration agreement, and these nations permit a second category of arbitration or conciliation not subject to such control should the parties so desire. Arbitrators of this latter kind are sometimes referred to as " amiables compositeurs." Finally, a third group of nations treats all arbitration as being in this latter class, with arbitrators under no obligation to decide according to law. For an authoritative comparative review of the position in different countries see Cohn in (1941) 4 U. of Tor.L.J. 1, though since that article and the Second World War there has been a tendency for a number of jurisdictions within the third and second groups to move towards a greater degree of control by the Courts.

Finally, English law has now been substantially altered while this Supplement is going to print, so as to permit international, as opposed to domestic, arbitrations conducted in England to reach their decisions free of judicial control by the Courts in appropriate cases should the proper law so require. The Act has also drastically modified the procedure by which control is exercised over the law administered in domestic arbitrations by abolishing the Case Stated procedure, and substituting a system of " speaking awards " in which arbitrators are required to state their reasons for their awards in much the same way as judges—see the Arbitration Act 1979: this should enable the courts to receive appeals on points of law more simply and effectively than under the Case Stated procedure.

819 **Agreements to refer.** These are usually expressed in mandatory language—"shall be referred." Failure to use such language has been held in Canada to render the claim unenforceable.

ILLUSTRATION

Clause 10 of a contract made the engineer's decisions as to the contract documents binding "subject always to arbitration." Clause 21 gave a right to determine on failure to pay "any sum certified by the engineer or awarded by arbitrators." Clause 22 gave indemnities, and provided that claims under this provision "shall be adjusted by agreement or arbitration." Clause 28 provided that in the event of a dispute either party "may be entitled to give . . . notice of such dispute and to request arbitration thereof." *Held* by the Saskatchewan Court of Appeal (Hall J.A. dissenting), following the Ontario Court of Appeal's decision in *Re McNamara Construction of Ontario Ltd. and Brock University* (1970) 11 D.L.R. (3d) 513, this was not a binding submission to arbitration within the Saskatchewan Arbitration Act 1965: *Re Fischbach and Moore of Canada* v. *Noranda Mines* (1971) 19 D.L.R. (3d) 329.

[*Note*: It is difficult not to feel sympathy with Hall J.A.'s dissenting judgment in the above case. Hall J.A. considered the words "request" and "may" were nothing more than a polite way of indicating the steps to be taken, and also pointed out that the contrary view meant that the other references to arbitration in the contract became meaningless. The Ontario *McNamara* case was a decision on clause 44 of a standard form of construction contract with identical words, but followed by the additional words "and the parties may with respect to the particular matters then in dispute agree to submit the same to arbitration." The two decisions, of course, mean that the clauses in question could as well have been omitted from the contract and that they had no significance whatever.]

Section 27 extension of time. See for this discretionary entitlement as a substantive matter involving the interpretation of the arbitration clause, and so governed by the proper law of the contract, and not a procedural matter governed by the *lex fori*, *International Tank and Pipe Ltd.* v. *Kuwait Aviation Fuelling* [1975] 1 Lloyd's Rep. 8. See also *Consolidated Investment & Contracting Co.* v. *Saponaria Shipping Co. Ltd.* (*The Virgo*) [1978] 3 All E.R. 988.

821 **Note to Kollberg case.** Word "no" is omitted in error in sentence "there are decisions and dicta to the contrary," and should be inserted before "decisions."

822 **First paragraph.** In the *Davies Middleton and Davies* case the Court of Appeal assumed that a power to appoint the arbitrator existed under section 10 of the Act, but in *National Enterprises* v. *Racal Communications* [1975] Ch. 397 the Court of Appeal held that they in fact had no power to do so, on the wording of section 10, in a case where the President of a professional institution had refused to appoint, and where the President was not an appointer in default of agreement.

Footnote 14. Further reference to *Davies* case should be to (1964) 62 L.G.R. 134.

825 **Miller case.** Reference now is to [1970] A.C. 583. The majority of the House of Lords did not rely on the subsequent conduct of the parties as relevant to the question of the proper law of the contract. The conduct relied on after the arbitrator's appointment in regard to procedure included correspondence with a " clerk to arbiter " on behalf of the arbitrator, in which discussion took place as to whether various matters were " in accordance with Scottish procedure."

829 **Chambers v. Goldthorpe.** See now *Sutcliffe* v. *Thakrah* [1974] A.C. 727 and *Arenson* v. *Casson Beckman* [1977] A.C. 405, and the discussion of these cases *ante* in this Supplement under pp. 165–169.

830 **Pierce v. Dyke.** Contrast, however, the leading case of *Doleman* v. *Ossett*, illustrated at p. 832 of the Tenth Edition, where the words " with or without formal reference or notice to the parties " appear to have attracted no attention.

SECTION 2. THE EFFECT OF THE ARBITRATION AGREEMENT

831 **Section 2.** See the new preliminary remarks on the English law of arbitration *supra* in this Supplement under p. 818.

837 **Insert further illustration** after illustration (4) and renumber (5) and later illustrations:

(5) The specification of a railway contract referred any dispute as to the meaning of the specification, or as to the adjustment or terms of the later contract under seal or as to " *usual or necessary claims* " or any other matter connected with the later contract to the owner's engineer as arbiter. *Held* by the First Division of the Court of Session, when a company sought to make its own engineer arbiter to determine disputes, the Court should interpret the clause strictly, and a claim for late information in which fault was imputed to the engineer was not within the clause: *McAlpine*

v. *Lancashire etc. Railway Co.* (1889) 27 *Scottish Law Reporter* 81.

839 Add further illustrations:

(14) Clause 33 of a lease provided that " any dispute . . . as to the rights duties or obligations hereunder or as to the meaning . . . of any of the terms and provisions hereof or as to any matter arising out of or concerning this agreement " should be referred to arbitration. The tenant claimed rectification of a clause regulating the adjustment of the rent by the insertion of certain words claimed to have been omitted by a common mistake. *Held* by the Appellate Division of the Supreme Court of South Africa, and not following the *Printing Machinery Co.* v. *Linotype Machinery* and *Crane* v. *Hegeman Harris* cases, that when the parties signed the lease they must have believed that it contained what they had in fact agreed upon, *i.e.* their real agreement, and when in clause 33 they used the words " this agreement," " rights duties and obligations hereunder " and " provisions hereof " they intended to refer to the agreement which they thought had been embodied in the document. It followed that a dispute about what any term of that agreement was arose out of or concerned the agreement. To hold otherwise would mean that a dispute about subsequent verbal or separate written variations of the agreement, or about a subsequent release or estoppel or waiver or set-off, would also have to be considered a dispute outside the document, and therefore not referable to arbitration: *Kathmer Investments* v. *Woolworths* [1970] 2 S.A.L.R. 498.

[*Note*: This outstanding decision injects, it is submitted, both commonsense and first principles into what had, in the English cases, become a legalistic and unconsidered dogma leading to the inconvenience and expense of separate proceedings in the courts, as well as defeating the obvious intentions of the parties to the contract as expressed in the language they had used in the arbitration clause. It is unreservedly to be welcomed on both legal and practical grounds.]

(15) A charter-party provided that " any dispute arising during execution of this charter-party " was to be settled by arbitration. Charterers twice arrested a ship, first in Amsterdam, then in Rotterdam, on a wrong view of the owners' rights under the charter-party. The owners' damages included claims in tort for the wrongful arrests. The Rotterdam arrest took place after the charter-party had been completed when the ship was under charter to other persons. *Held* by the Court of Appeal, the umpire had jurisdiction, since though both claims were in tort and the second arose from events after the charter-party was ended, the first arrest was so closely connected with the dispute arising out of the contract that it came within the arbitration clause, and the second arrest was so much part and parcel of the original dispute that it would be absurd to deny the umpire jurisdiction to dispose of all claims at the same time: *The Damianos* [1971] 2 Q.B. 588.

Step in the proceedings. In their enthusiasm to find that a step has been taken, some of the English cases on this subject appear excessively legalistic and to have lost sight of the underlying principle, which can only be, it is submitted, to avoid prejudice to the plaintiff resisting arbitration should he be likely to have altered his position to his detriment as a result of the "step" taken by the party seeking arbitration.

Footnote 99. Add: see also *Building and Engineering Construction* v. *Property Security* [1960] V.R. 673.

841   **Add further illustrations:**

(2) The plaintiff had been reduced to poverty by the alleged breaches, and had obtained legal aid. If a stay was granted, the legal aid would have to cease, since it was not available in arbitrations. *Held* by the Court of Appeal, a stay would be refused: *Fakes* v. *Taylor Woodrow Construction* [1973] Q.B. 436.

[*Note:* This case may, perhaps, be regarded as near the limits of any possible legal discretion but serves to indicate the wide scope of the English Courts' discretion under section 4.]

(3) A building owner brought an action for defects against the builder. The writ was just in time from the point of view of limitation. The builder applied for a stay. The owner objected that the effect would be to deprive him of his remedy, since the limitation period had now expired, and for purposes of limitation the arbitration would date from the day of the stay being granted. The builder replied that by reason of the late issue of the writ he himself was in danger of having limitation successfully pleaded against him by a number of sub-contractors who had actually done the work, while being himself liable to the owner. *Held* by Bean J., a stay should be refused so as to allow the plaintiff the advantage of his writ, but on terms that the builder issue third party proceedings against the sub-contractors, and if limitation be raised successfully on a preliminary issue in any of those proceedings (with the plaintiff participating in those proceedings on that issue) then the plaintiff should to that extent discontinue his own proceedings against the defendant: *County and District Properties* v. *Jenner* [1976] 2 Lloyd's Rep. 728.

[*Note*: The above facts are all disclosed in Swanwick J.'s later judgment on the limitation issues when explaining its earlier history. For the case in relation to the limitation issues see *supra* in this Supplement under p. 306.]

843   **Footnote 25.** The *Absalom* case was concerned with setting aside an award for *an error of law on its face*, where it will be seen that the same distinction between "agreements to refer" and specific submissions of questions of law is made.

844   **Insert illustration** after second paragraph.

ILLUSTRATION

A seller gave a buyer two letters of indemnity in England, as a result of which the buyer paid certain invoiced amounts to third parties. The buyer issued a writ claiming damages under the indemnities, and later amended to allege breach of the contract of sale. The sale notes had provided that all disputes were to be arbitrated in Pakistan and subject to Pakistani law. The seller applied for a stay. *Held* by Mocatta J., refusing a stay, there was a danger of inconsistent findings of fact and holdings in law if the issues were split between the English action on the indemnities and the arbitration in Pakistan. It was unlikely that Pakistani law would differ substantially from English law, and on the balance of convenience all issues should be decided in England: *Brazendale & Co.* v. *Saint Freres* [1970] 2 Lloyd's Rep. 34.

SECTION 3. DISQUALIFICATION OF ARBITRATORS

849 Misconduct: Warning should perhaps be given that the expression " misconduct " is used somewhat freely by the courts in a class of cases where all that is really involved is an error of law, and no blameworthy conduct is involved. The advantage of finding such " technical " misconduct is that it arguably widens the statutory powers of the courts to intervene and maintain supervision over arbitrators who have " misconducted " themselves, which is a tendency to be encouraged and welcomed in the interests of all parties.

852 Add illustrations:

(21) The arbitrator wrote that he would view before the hearing. The claimant conducted his case on the basis that there would be a view, calling no expert evidence. The arbitrator did not in fact view before his award. *Held* by Park J., that there had been misconduct within section 23 (2), and the award should be set aside: *Micklewright* v. *Mullock* (1974) 232 E.G. 337; [1975] C.L.Y. 107.

(22) An arbitrator refused to award interest, though asked to do so. *Held* by Kerr J., it was technical misconduct to do so where sufficient facts were before the arbitrator for the purpose: *Van Der Zijden Wildhandel NV* v. *Tucker & Cross* [1976] 1 Lloyd's Rep. 341. (See also the *Marples Ridgeway* case at pp. 867–868 of the Tenth Edition.)

Power of court to appoint. For a lacuna in this power in the case of a named appointor refusing to appoint, see *National Enterprises Ltd.* v. *Racal Communications* [1975] 1 W.L.R. 222 (as opposed to refusal by appointor named in default of agreement, which will be covered by Section 10).

SECTION 4. ARBITRATION CONDITION PRECEDENT TO ACTION

854 Add further illustration: *S.A. Railways* v. *Egan* (1973) 47 A.L.J.R. 140, illustration (13) *ante* in this Supplement under p. 446.

Footnote 79. Add: For mere non-payment not a dispute, see *L.N.W.R.* v. *Billington* [1899] A.C. 79. Contrast and distinguish the *Ramac* case illustrated *supra* in this Supplement under p. 639 (non-payment for a disputed reason).

855 **A second class of cases** where the parties may lose their rights both to arbitration and litigation are the " time bar " cases, where arbitration is made conditional upon notice of claim or arbitration being given within a stipulated time (" Atlantic Shipping " clauses as they are known, to distinguish them from other similar clauses which may bar arbitration but leave the right to litigation unimpaired—see *Russell on Arbitration* (18th ed.), pp. 58–60) subject to the possible mitigating effect of the very conservatively exercised power to extend time under such clauses in the " undue hardship " section 27 of the Act. See also the *International Tank* case referred to *supra* in this Supplement under p. 819 for the substantive effect of that section in international arbitrations where the contract is governed by English law.

SECTION 5. PROCEDURE IN ARBITRATIONS

857 **Section 27 (3) Limitation Act.** The anomaly whereby this section applies without modification to arbitrations which arise as a result of an action in the courts being stayed, whereupon the plaintiff loses the benefit of the date of his writ, has already been mentioned in this Supplement under pp. 818 and 841.
R.I.B.A. forms. Now radically amended in this respect—see the new clause 30 (7).

858 **Farr's case.** See the discussion and further authorities referred to *supra* in this Supplement under p. 495.

859 **Footnote 95.** Add: (a case of an application in respect of an insolvent limited company under s. 447 of the Companies Act).
Footnote 96. Add: see *Kursell* v. *Timber Operators* [1923] 2 K.B. 202.

863 **Sealed offers.** The practice is touched upon by McNair J., in *Demolition and Construction Ltd.* v. *Kent River Board* [1963] 2 Lloyd's Rep. 7 at p. 16 and in *Dineen* v. *Walpole* [1969] 1 Lloyd's Rep. 261.

864 **Arbitrators** should also not hesitate to take legal advice if specific legal problems whether procedural or substantive become urgent during the hearing, or before making their award—particularly, of course, if asked to state a special Case. The restrictions on taking legal advice, in cases where there has not been a specific submission of a point of law (to which different considerations will apply) but where the point simply arises during the course of the case in the usual way, have perhaps been somewhat overstated in *Russell on Arbitration* (18th ed.), pp. 196–197.

Statement of Case. First sentence and footnote 6. See for the general principles governing the ordering of a special case, *The Lysland* [1973] 1 Lloyd's Rep. 296. Unless the case falls within recognised exceptions (*e.g.* a specific submission of a point of law to the arbitrator) an arbitrator will normally be compelled to do so on any clear-cut bona fide point of law (*Halfdan Grieg* v. *Sterling Coal* ("*The Lysland*") [1973] Q.B. 843). See now, however, the Arbitration Act 1979, which has abolished the Case Stated procedure.

865 **Add at end of first paragraph:** For the extent to which the arbitrator should review evidence or state or make findings of fact in his case see *Tersons* v. *Stevenage* [1965] 1 Q.B. 37, and *Russell on Arbitration* (18th ed.), pp. 250–251. For the distinction between primary and secondary findings of fact see *ibid*, and for a striking example of this, *Peak Construction Co.* v. *McKinney Foundations* (1971) 69 L.G.R. 1 (*primary* findings of fact, if statute or principle require it, may bind an appellate tribunal, but secondary findings (*i.e.* inferences from the primary facts, generally will not).

The foregoing remarks must now, however, be regarded as subject to the new system of "separate awards" called for by the Arbitration Act 1979 in the case of domestic arbitrations.

Add further illustration:

(2) A contractor sued for amounts due on an interim certificate. The building owner defended on *quantum*, but as an alternative pleaded a termination subsequent to the certificate, and that in consequence under the terms of the contract nothing was due in any event. By agreement there was no hearing, and the arbitrator was asked to decide on the documents. The arbitrator found for the contractor, and stated a case which made no mention of the alternative defence. The building owner did not take up the special case within the permitted period, but resisted enforcement of the award on the ground that there had been a mistake of law. *Held* by the Court of Appeal, the arbitrator had impliedly

found against the alternative defence and the award should be enforced: *Middlemiss & Gould* v. *Hartlepool Corporation* [1972] 1 W.L.R. 1643.

867 **Separation of award from order for costs.** There is no reason why this should depend on the request or agreement of the parties. The arbitrator can either make his final award without mentioning costs, leaving it to the parties to apply for an order for costs within the period permitted under section 18 (4) of the Act (which expressly contemplates final awards that do not deal with costs), or else he can make his award expressly as an interim award under section 14 without mentioning costs, and deal with costs in a final award after hearing the parties' submissions.

868 **Action upon the award.** This in fact is only used in a disputed case. In straightforward cases direct enforcement of the award under section 26 of the Act is the appropriate remedy.

870 **Insert further illustration** after first paragraph of text:

(2) In a dispute between owners and charterers as to responsibility for insect infestation of cargo, the umpire held the owners not to blame and so awarded. He ordered them to pay their own costs, and half of the costs of the award. *Held* by Mocatta J., there were no grounds, in the judicial exercise of the arbitrator's discretion, for departing from the general principle that costs follow the event; that while not obliged to state his reasons when departing from the general rule, it would in most cases save costs if he stated his reasons in his award—in that event the parties would be saved the expense of trying to ascertain his reasons and possibly moving to set aside the award; and that if no reasons were stated the party objecting to the award might bring before the Court such evidence as he could obtain as to the grounds or lack of grounds: *L. Figueiredo Navegacas S.A.* v. *The Erich Schroeder* [1974] 1 Lloyd's Rep. 192.

INDEX TO SUPPLEMENT

Page references are to pages of main work as cited in margin of Supplement.
Readers should also consult main Index.

INDEX TO SUPPLEMENT